D1311348

ROB LONG was co-executive producer of *Cheers* for its
eleventh and final season. Together with his writing partner,
Dan Staley, he co-created and co-executive-produced the
series *Pig Sty* and *Good Company*.

ROB LONG

Conversations with My Agent

A PLUME BOOK

PLUME
Published by the Penguin Group
Penguin Putnam Inc., 375 Hudson Street, New York, New York 10014, U.S.A.
Penguin Books Ltd, 27 Wrights Lane, London W8 5TZ, England
Penguin Books Australia Ltd, Ringwood, Victoria, Australia
Penguin Books Canada Ltd, 10 Alcorn Avenue, Toronto, Ontario, Canada M4V 3B2
Penguin Books (N.Z.) Ltd, 182–190 Wairau Road, Auckland 10, New Zealand

Penguin Books Ltd, Registered Offices: Harmondsworth, Middlesex, England

Published by Plume, an imprint of Dutton NAL,
a member of Penguin Putnam Inc.
Previously published in a Dutton edition.

First Plume Printing, July, 1998
10 9 8 7 6 5 4 3 2 1

 REGISTERED TRADEMARK—MARCA REGISTRADA

The Library of Congress has catalogued the Dutton edition as follows:
Long, Rob.
    Conversations with my agent / Rob Long.
        p.   cm.
    ISBN 0-525-94222-X (hc.)
    ISBN 0-452-27713-2 (pbk.)
    1. Long, Rob.   2. Television producers—United States—Biography.
3. Television writers—United States—Biography.   I. Title.
PN1992.4.L66A3   1997
791.45'0232'092—dc20   96–26958
    [B]   CIP

Printed in the United States of America

BOOKS ARE AVAILABLE AT QUANTITY DISCOUNTS WHEN USED TO PROMOTE PRODUCTS
OR SERVICES. FOR INFORMATION PLEASE WRITE TO PREMIUM MARKETING DIVISION,
PENGUIN PUTNAM INC., 375 HUDSON STREET, NEW YORK, NEW YORK 10014.

THANKS

to my parents,
for their patience;

to my agent, Beth Uffner,
who resembles the agent in this book in only two respects:
she always tells the truth, and she gives excellent advice;

to Toby Young,
editor of the late *Modern Review*;

but mostly to my writing partner, Dan Staley,
the most talented writer I know.

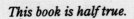

This book is half true.

Bottoms Up

FADE IN: SPRING 1993

I am a co-executive producer of the long-running, phenomenally successful television series *Cheers*. My writing partner, Dan Staley, and I have risen rapidly through the staff-writing ranks since 1990, when we drove onto the Paramount Studios lot in my decrepit rust heap of a ten-year-old Subaru (bought in New Hampshire for eight hundred dollars; 72,340 miles on the odometer; strange, acrid-sweet smell wafting from the front end during left turns), and began our careers in television. I am a know-it-all twenty-seven years old, and from my tiny mountaintop, two years on *Cheers* meant a lifetime. A career. *Cheers*, the IBM of television shows.

Last December, Ted Danson, star of the show, meal ticket for hundreds (including me), the man who portrayed Sam Malone—rogue bartender, ladies' man, athlete—decides, "What the hell, time to move on."

So I do what you do when you work in Hollywood and something bad happens. I call my agent. An hour or two later, my agent calls back.

CUT TO:

INT. LUCILLE BALL BUILDING, PARAMOUNT
STUDIOS—DAY

MY AGENT (OVER PHONE)
What do you want?

ME
You called me.

MY AGENT
I did?

Pause.
SFX: Papers rattling.

MY AGENT (CONT'D)
Oh yeah. Listen, the show's not coming back.

ME
I know.

MY AGENT
I know you know. I was just *reiterating* for convenience. Listen, you and Dan are in a good position right now. There's a lot of heat on [my agent mentions a famous Hollywood actor] to do a series with you guys at the helm. There's just one fly in the ointment, but otherwise, you guys should take the meeting.

ME
What's the fly in the ointment?

MY AGENT
What are you talking about?

ME
You said that there's a fly in the ointment.

MY AGENT
There's no fly in the ointment.

ME

But you just said—

MY AGENT

The fly in the ointment is that they need a
script by the end of the month.

ME

It's the nineteenth.

MY AGENT

I think your obsession with dates is
unhealthy.

ME

Hmmmmm.

MY AGENT

This is grown-up time, boys. It's a cold
world out there. *Cheers* is *fini*. Think it
over.

SFX: Click. Dial tone.

CUT TO:

A few months later, the script is unwritten, the famous Hollywood actor's interest in us and television is history, and we are
contemplating signing a "development deal" with a large studio.
Another conversation with my agent—this one in person:

EXT. PATIO—ORSO'S RESTAURANT—DAY

MY AGENT

Good news. You've got a pilot
commitment from the network.

ME

Wow. Great! What does that mean?

MY AGENT

Nothing.

ME
So why is it good news?

Beat. Rolling eyes in my direction. A "why-do-I-have-to-put-up-with-this" take to the waiter.

MY AGENT
It's good news because it means you're a player. It means that when you approach the studio for an overall deal, you have something to bring to the party. You can bargain from a position of strength.

ME
Great! Does that mean more money?

MY AGENT
Definitely not. You're in a very weak position.

ME
But I thought you said—

MY AGENT
Look, it's not 1989, okay? There's no development money around. It's nineteen-fucking-ninety-three. Everything's different. I mean, my God, there's no Berlin Wall anymore. Do you want to turn back the clock? Is that it?

ME
But I thought you said—

MY AGENT
Things are tough. What I said was *Things are tough.*

CUT TO:

A development deal is one of those entertainment-industry creations that, when described, sound suspiciously like goofing off. Essentially, the studio agrees to pay a writer a minimum sum over two years, hopeful that the writer, once the novelty of being paid good money—sometimes, great money—to do absolutely nothing but sit and think wears off and he's thoroughly disgusted with a workday that begins at eleven in the morning and ends roughly after lunch, will just decide, "What the hell, I may as well create a hit television show."

The reason these deals last two years is that it takes at least one year for the writer to become tired of moseying into the office at eleven, and skulking out at one-thirty. Or so I'm told. My personal mission, over the next two years, is to test that particular old wives' tale.

The development deal was signed March 1993, to take effect on June 1. Signed, of course, is a not quite accurate term. No piece of paper was actually produced, you see; no contract drawn up. In Hollywood, written—that is to say, legally binding—contracts are thought of as vulgar. In fact, just asking for a written contract is apt to bring out the latent *mafiosi* in Industry denizens. "I'm giving you my word," their pained expressions seem to say. "What? You don't *trust* me?"

And besides, the actual document—thirty pages long, perhaps, and cast in language sadistically designed to render generally accepted accounting phrases like "profit" and "loss" and "guarantee" into "numerically impossible" and "insurmountable" and "yeah, *right*"—is a sheaf of papers that will be tied up in dense, expensive legal wrangling for the duration of the two-year term of the deal itself. And since almost all of the wrangling centers around what the colorful phrasemakers who run things in this town like to call "the back end" (i.e. syndication money, overseas sales, reruns, spin-offs, video games, toys, whatever), and since any "back end" money is way, way, way in the fuzzy distance, there's no particular rush to settle the issues once and for all, certainly not for the lawyers, who have second houses to buy and children's tuition to pay. So the "back end" just sits there, waiting. The two schools of thought among writers are, one: "No matter what, *don't let the studio screw you in the back end*"; and two: "Hey, you may not have a back end at all, so tell the studio—*if you pay me a lot of money now, I'll let you screw me in the back end.*"

So one settles for a "deal memo"—one sheet of paper that lists the key elements of the deal: money, title, office requirements, parking—I'm serious—and a secretary. In short, the five pillars of happiness for the 818, 213, and 310 telephone area codes.

In fact, the only problem with a development deal is that almost everyone in Hollywood has one. That kind of mitigates its prestige. There is even a sardonic term for it: "development hell," which refers to the endless round of meetings and adjustments that the studio or the network (or, worst-case scenario, the studio *and* the network) demand of one's original script or idea. Since they've got you for two years, they reckon, they may as well stretch every decision out exactly that long. Thus follows one of the Industry's most immutable rules: time constraints—due to star availability, network time slot, opening dates, whatever—always work in the writer's favor. The less time you have, the less meddlesome the studio and networks can be.

Sadly, the reverse is also true.

At the final wrap party for the eleventh and last season of *Cheers*, I was staring blankly in the distance, drink in hand, listening to the band, Los Lobos, play. It was a quiet, reflective moment. I thought about the last few months of the show, the camaraderie, the friendships, the emotion of saying good-bye. And I also thought about the gifts. The crystal beer mugs; the gold pins; the signed Hirschfeld etchings; the director's chairs. And I thought about the parties. Not just this one, but the penultimate show party. The bottles of Cristal; the Cohiba Esplendidos; the grilled shrimp; the Beluga. And the media attention. The interviews; the profiles; the constant refrain, in every article, in every interview: "It's the writing, really. It's all in the writing. . . ." The actors, who, by that time, had certainly earned the right (by Hollywood standards, at least) to be cranky and inflexible and insane, were unflappably charming and professional—no diva scenes, no trailer wars. And I realized that not once during my tenure on the show—not once—did the network or the studio say, "No, you can't do that." Oh, occasionally they would call and ask us, pretty please, not to say "Up your ass" or "She's a bitch," and we would always comply. But mostly we were left alone. Nobody thought too much about us. *Cheers* just was.

My thoughts were interrupted by the approach of a studio executive, who also had a drink in his hand. A big drink. And not his first.

"Thinking about the good times?" he asked.

I nodded.

"Think all you want. They're over. You and your partner are just development schmucks now."

He laughed merrily, clapped me on the back, and hustled over to the bar.

Uh-oh.

A few days later I got a call from a publicity person. She wanted to know whether I would be attending the party in Boston on May 20 (yes, this would be the third party) to celebrate the broadcast of the final episode. I'm from Boston, you see, and in the show's previous visits—to shoot location footage or bits of exterior scenes—I've always been trotted out by the publicity people as the local boy, available, as they say in the trade, for interviews. That no one, to date, had yet taken them up on the offer made no difference. The publicity person wanted to know if I was going, and would I be available for interviews.

I thought about this: a round-trip, first-class ticket; a suite at the Ritz; a generous expense account with which to take all my pals from Boston to dinner. Everything like it was on my previous visits with the show. "Yes," I thought, "yes I said yes yes."

She must have heard me ordering room service in my thoughts.

"This will all be at your own expense, of course. I just wanted to know if you were planning to be there anyway, to visit your parents or something. You could drop by the party, maybe do an interview, whatever. Let me know."

Click. Dial tone.

Uh-oh.

I spent the first week of May fly-fishing in Northern California, and the last three weeks traveling in Hong Kong and Vietnam. On May 20, the date of the last *Cheers* broadcast, I was in a bar in Halong Bay, in North Vietnam, drinking Vietnamese beer and eating boiled crab. I went there at my own expense, of course, and did no interviews. I returned home to a different planet. I landed at LAX, headed through customs, and was quickly shuttled to the "Guy in Development" line.

Going out to dinner in Los Angeles, so simple two months before, now became slightly harder. Before, one simply asked a production secretary to call up the restaurant and book a table for seven o'clock. (People eat early in Los Angeles.) No two-days-in-advance, no I'll-see-what-I-can-do, just a crisp "No problem, we'll see you at seven o'clock."

Restaurants always ask for a telephone number to "confirm your reservation," or so they say. What they really want to do is check up on you, to make sure that you are who you say you are. Otherwise, any old grubby film student can call the Ivy, say, and book a table for Mr. Eisner, show up, and politely explain, after being seated, that Mr. Eisner was unaccountably detained. I know this for a fact. I once was a grubby film student. The important thing, when giving your number, is to give them the right three-digit exchange: Paramount is 956, Disney 560, Tri-Star 280, and the others, well, I don't know the others. Ask my production secretary. When I get one. When I get into production.

The point is, when you've got an office and you're in production, you get a table. Otherwise, it's "We can fit you in at five-forty-five or nine-thirty."

It's now the beginning of July. Dan and I are beginning the process of developing our own series. We are having dinner with our agent next week. The conversation went something like this:

CUT TO:

INT. MY HOUSE—DAY

> MY AGENT (OVER PHONE)
> Let's have dinner. We need to talk.

> ME
> But we *are* talking.

> MY AGENT
> I mean in person. I mean in *reality*.

> ME
> Oh.

> MY AGENT
> This is development, okay? I'll be in your
> face until you're in production.

Uh-oh.

> ME
> Um . . . okay. Dinner sounds fine. How
> about Morton's at eight?

> MY AGENT
> Good.

> ME
> I'll call and make the reservation.

> MY AGENT
> No, *I'll* call and make the reservation. You
> won't get one.

> ME
> Wow.

MY AGENT
That's life.

ME
I know. I'm just remembering a time when
I could easily get a table, when I was an
important person.

MY AGENT
I've got some news for you, sweetheart.
You were *never* an important person. The
show was important. The *show* got the
table. You were just some guy.

ME
Wow.

MY AGENT
You want to be important? Create a show
of your own. Get a hit on the air. Then
you'll be important.

ME
Wow.

MY AGENT
And the only way you get a show on the
air is to do a little work. That means
showing up before eleven and staying past
two. See you at Morton's.

SFX: Click. Dial tone.
Uh-oh. Uh-oh. Uh-oh.

FADE OUT.

Flashback

FADE IN: SEPTEMBER 1988

I drove into Los Angeles for the first time on Labor Day, 1988—the hottest day of the year, air yellowed by smog and ozone, rattling into town from Las Vegas in an eight-year-old Subaru station wagon, my back sticking to the seat—and wanted nothing less than to fall in love with the city at once. I had driven clear across the country—six days of heat and highway—heading for film school at UCLA; I was twenty-three, and was still young enough to think that one's first glimpse of a city would create a lasting and meaningful impression.

What I glimpsed, coming over the hill on the 10 Freeway, was downtown Los Angeles. Downtown is where banks, investment houses, big accountancies, consultancies, oil company head-quarters, and other adult-run and -managed concerns make their offices. Downtown has nothing to do with the Industry, except in a vaguely peripheral way. In the six years I have lived in Los Angeles, not counting that first passing through, I have been to downtown Los Angeles precisely five times.

Later that week, after I had moved into a small room in a large house in Brentwood, I learned a bit about Los Angeles geography, and its complicated class system: Pasadena and San Marino are on the east side of downtown, have an old-money, old-line, aristocratic bearing due to the large numbers of East Coast millionaires that moved west in the first half of the century for—get this—the clean, dry air; Hollywood, high on the hills above Sunset Boulevard, is a maze of zigzaggy roads and treacherous turns—deadly to those who enjoy a generous cocktail hour—with nutty, rambling houses peopled by Industry types, rock-star types, foreign types, and drug-dealer types; moving south and west, West Hollywood is the center of the Gay Universe, its surrounding areas the Young Industry Assistant and Production Assistant Ghetto, where all the young aspirants to agent/executive/producerhood live; then Beverly Hills (enough said); then Bel Air (shh); then across the great divide, the 405 Freeway, heading into the Haute West Side—Brentwood, Pacific Palisades, and where I now reside, Santa Monica—places rich and cool, sophisticated, beach-centered, casual, child-friendly, and Industry-heavy with actors, lawyers, television writers, top-line agents, studio executives, and doctors. Over the hills is the Valley, which, no matter how big the houses get or how rich the inhabitants, remains utterly and always "the Valley."

People who live across the Great Divide, the 405 Freeway, maintain that the air is smogless (smog, presumably, respectfully clinging to the airspace above the cheaper, less fashionable parts of town) and that the temperature is ten degrees cooler. People who live across the Great Divide rarely, if ever, venture beyond the border at night. They eat "in the neighborhood," which, while it often entails a fifteen- or twenty-minute drive, generously encompasses the Brentwood/Palisades/Santa Monica area as it ruthlessly excludes all points east of the 405. It is not uncommon to see two studio chiefs and a network president or two, all shopping at the Gelson's supermarket in the Palisades on a Saturday, all with children in tow, out of their slick suits and into sweatpants and T-shirts, all the ruthlessness and power drained from their bodies in the face of four children, three of whom each want a different kind of cereal, and one of whom has to go to the bathroom, *right now, Daddy! Right now!*

So it wasn't my first glimpse of the city that made me think, "Okay, I can live here." It was the rich hustle and bustle of Gelson's, the huge tower of perfect oranges and emerald green lettuces, the dazzling six kinds of apples and pears from Washington State (each in its own Styrofoam valise), and the short Mexican man, standing at a huge orange press, ready to squeeze a gallon of fresh orange juice for the asking. (In general, of course, it is the ubiquitous short Mexican man who makes Los Angeles livable at all: he squeezes the juice, tends the garden, washes and parks the car, and clears your table at the restaurant, pretending not to hear you while you complain that "the illegal immigrants are ruining this city!")

A few days later, I started film school.

CUT TO:

INT. UCLA CLASSROOM—DAY

I file in with two dozen other writerish-looking folks, all of us in the Master of Fine Arts (a master's degree! for writing movies!) in Screenwriting Program in the School of Theatre, Film, and Television (notice what comes last?) at UCLA. We take our seats.

The head of the program, a bearded, elfin-looking guy in pressed jeans and a white shirt, greets us.

HEAD OF PROGRAM
(*passing out sheets*)
I'm passing out a list of the scripts I've
written, and the subsequent events that
led to me getting cheated out of screen
credit. The important thing, though, isn't
the list of scripts I wrote, but the book I
wrote on scriptwriting, which will be the
text for this class, and which is available at
all of the big bookstores, for $22.95. Okay?
Buy the book. Class dismissed.

Between now and the middle of December (roughly three and a half months) there are only nine class meetings scheduled, of which this one, lasting all of ten minutes, is the first.

DISSOLVE TO:

INT. UCLA CLASSROOM—DAY

I have been in film school several months. What I have learned is: the first ten pages of a screenplay are important; the teachers in the program who aren't writing movies are writing books about writing movies; two classes a week, an hour and a half apiece, leaves me plenty of free time; and at this rate, I will never get my MFA.

In this particular class, we are required to present the first ten pages of our current scripts. I have just presented mine.

CLASSMATE #1

I like it.

CLASSMATE #2

Yeah. I like it too.

CLASSMATE #1

But isn't there too much dialogue? I mean, all that talking and talking and talking.

ME

Yeah, I guess it's kind of talky.

CLASSMATE #2

You know what it is? It's *television*. That's what it is.

It takes me quite a long time to realize that this was meant as an insult.

CUT TO:

The truth is, I knew I was writing television all along. But they don't have any television classes at film school. They have classes *about* television ("Mass Media in the Age of Reagan: Plugged In and Tuned Out" and "Video Texts: MTV, Madonna, and Strategies of Discourse"), but they don't have any classes about how to *do* television.

And again, the truth is, I had wanted to do television all along. Dan and I met as Yale undergraduates. We wrote two plays together, mounted two successful productions, and had made a rough pact to eventually try our hands at Hollywood. Our timing was a bit off: I am two years younger, and so was finishing up my final years at Yale while he was beginning a very promising career in advertising, but other than that, we were on track.

Two years before, in my final year in college, we took a stab at sitcom writing. Someone told us (most stories about early failures begin with the words "Someone told me . . .") that we needed to write an episode of a then-popular show, *Newhart*, get it to someone in the business, and we'd be flown out to LA and never look back. So we wrote a *Newhart* script, called a "spec" script for two reasons: one, it's short for "speculative"; and two, because "spec" also describes the importance of the authors in the landscape of Hollywood. We polished up the script, sent it to a friend of a friend of a friend—a big-time, old-line TV-writing veteran—and we waited for the messenger to bring us the plane tickets to take us away.

What we got back, instead, was our script. Covered in notes and pencil marks, and appended to it, this note:

CUT TO:

INSERT SHOT: NOTE ON SCRIPT

Rob's trembling fingers clutch the note. It reads:

> This is the worst spec script I've ever read in
> 15 years of reading these things. You've made
> the main character totally unlikable!!! There's
> no moment at the end!!! Terrible. Just terrible.

CUT TO:

INSERT SHOT: THE SCRIPT

Rob's whitened fingers flip through the pages of the script. He stops at a bit of dialogue, next to it this penciled note:

no no no No No NO NO NO!

CUT TO:

So, off I went to film school, to discover, if possible, what we had done wrong. What I discovered was this: for all the hype and fantasy that centers around "breaking into the business," the simple truth is, for television writing anyway, the more businesslike the approach, the more success it will garner. The sheer silliness of sending our *Newhart* spec to a friend of a friend of a friend was never more evident than when that friend three times removed decided, "What the hell," and took a giant crap on it.

No, the way to do it is simpler: write a couple specs (by that time, Dan and I had our *Newhart* and a *Murphy Brown*), send them to a bunch of agents, and wait.

Simpler, of course, in one way; much harder in another. The waiting part is easy, though nerve-wracking and infuriating. Getting the names of various agents is also trouble-free: a matter of calling up the Writers Guild and asking for the "agency department." It's the writing of the specs that's tricky. It has always amazed me how many people who are trying to break into the business declare: "Oh, I *know* my stuff is funny—that's not what I'm worried about—it's that I don't know anyone who knows anyone."

Not so fast, amigo.

CUT TO:

INT. MY (STUDENT) PLACE—DAY

I have identified three agents who specialize in television writers. Dan, three thousand miles away in New York, has decided to trust me in this particular phase of our career.

I am folding up a letter.

CUT TO:

INSERT SHOT: LETTER

My confident fingers hold up the letter for a final inspection. It reads:

> Dear [name of agent],
> My writing partner, Dan Staley, and I have written two spec scripts for television—a *Newhart* and a *Murphy Brown*. We are currently seeking representation.
> Dan and I met as Yale undergraduates and have been writing together ever since. I am an MFA student at the School of Theatre, Film, and Television at UCLA. Dan is a Clio Award–winning copywriter based in New York.
> Would you be interested in reading our work?
> I look forward to hearing from you soon.
> Sincerely,

I sign the letter with a flourish, seal it in an envelope, am about to affix a stamp, and then I think better of it. I'll hand deliver each letter today, right now. My day is free, after all. I do have a class, but that is several weeks away.

CUT TO:

INT. MY (STUDENT) PLACE—DAY

Later that afternoon. I am trying to decide which book to take to the beach, Barbara Tuchman's A Distant

Mirror *or Paul Johnson's* Modern Times. *(In my film school idleness, I have decided to catch up on my serious reading.)*
SFX: Phone rings.
I answer it.

ME
Hello?

FEMALE VOICE
Is this Rob Long or Dan Staley?

My heart goes into systolic/diastolic reverse.

ME
This is Rob.

FEMALE VOICE
Hi, this is [she gives her name]. I work for [she gives the name of one of the agents I sent my letter to—a major agent at a big agency] and we got your letter today, which was strange because it didn't even have a stamp on it—anyway, [she mentions the agent again] wants to read your specs.

ME
(quivery voice, trying to sound cool)
Great. Super. I'll send them.

FEMALE VOICE
Don't. I'll have a messenger pick them up this afternoon. Okay?

ME
Oh—

SFX: Click. Dial Tone.

I rush outside with the scripts and sit on the lawn, waiting for the messenger to pick up my future.

CUT TO:

INT. MY (STUDENT) PLACE—DAY

The next day. I am giddy with excitement. A big agent is reading our specs. Maybe he's reading them right now and chuckling to himself. Maybe he's going to call to ask me to lunch. Maybe he's assembling a huge team of agents to woo us with promises and flattery.

I get a grip. I think: "This is Thursday. He's going to wait until the weekend to read the specs, love them, and start our careers. So the smart, prudent, careful thing to do is call Dan in New York, tell him to quit his job today, now, fly out here ready to meet this guy Monday morning, Tuesday at the latest."

I pick up the phone to call Dan.
SFX: Doorbell.
I hang up the phone without dialing, cross to the door, open it.

The agency messenger is there. With a package roughly the size of two television scripts. I sign for it. Tear it open right there at the open front door. Our scripts come tumbling out.
With a note.

CUT TO:

INSERT SHOT: NOTE

Trembling fingers. Again. The note reads:

> Dear Dan and Rob,
>   Thank you very much for the opportunity to read your work. Although the writing has many fine points, I do not feel it is strong enough for me to give you the one hundred

percent enthusiasm that you deserve and that
this industry requires.

Sincerely,

And below that, the agent's name, typed.
No signature.
And below the typed name:

DICTATED BUT NOT READ

Yikes.

CUT TO:

Soon, after the initial sting wears off, I recover my compo-
sure. A friend from film school recommended a surefire
recovery technique: compile a comprehensive Enemies List,
placing that agent's name and the name of his assistant at the
very top, and swear a solemn vow to one day, one way, wreak a
terrible and bloody revenge. I find this suggestion immensely
useful, and a good deal cheaper than a huge bottle of bourbon.

One down, two to go. Both of the remaining agents have our
scripts. I dig a deep trench, fortify it with ammunition and
pointed sticks, and wait.

And, it turns out, wait.

I wait four weeks. Unable to wait any longer, I call Agent #2.

CUT TO:

INT. MY (STUDENT) PLACE—DAY

I am in my pajamas, on the phone. It is 11:00 a.m.
Since the messengered rejection note, I have let myself
fall into some bad habits. I explain who I am to the
agent's assistant, memorizing her name for possible
future inclusion in my Enemies List.

A pause. Suddenly the agent breaks into the conversation.

AGENT'S VOICE
I know why you're calling and I know

what you want but I've been very sick and I just haven't read the material yet, okay? I haven't read it. I've been sick, and I'm building a new house and that's just madness—*don't ever build a house! Just don't do it!*—and so, no I haven't read them, but yes, I am going to and what was your name again just so I have it?

ME

It's Rob L—

AGENT'S VOICE

Oh. Here it is in front of me.

SFX: Click. Dial Tone.

CUT TO:

In the end, of course, that agent's voice became *my* agent's voice. We signed the agency papers in early December 1989. By the middle of January 1990, we were preparing for our first meeting with the then-producers of *Cheers*. From there to a staff-writing job on the show, and three years later, we were co-executive producers.

It seems fast in retrospect—and it seemed fast then too—but the lucky break and the fast climb also followed a certain logic: we kept our head down and wrote our specs; we approached agents methodically, without tricks or cutesy letters; we made the right choice and signed with a no-bullshit, straight-talking agent without a trace of the schmoozer; and we were very, very, very lucky.

My film school career was truncated, of course, which disturbed my mother ("You may need a graduate degree to fall back on") but, oddly, *didn't* disturb the head of the graduate writing program ("Go! Get out of here! This is a trade school and you've found your trade! Now, git!").

The moment I withdrew from the screenwriting program, I

also withdrew from the posture that my time in Los Angeles was a dilettante's adventure. Eighteen months before, I had moved to a new city three thousand miles from home, to break into a notoriously closed and clannish business. What comforted me when the jitters came, when the what-am-I-doing-heres crept up, was a stack of law school applications by my bedside. Small comfort, I know; and yet there is nothing more wasteful or pathetic than trying to get invited to a party that simply won't have you—and I was terrified that a year or two would tick by, then a third, then a fourth, and still this elusive business would elude me. I'm a fold-your-tent person, a proponent of the strategic surrender and the cutting of losses. By this time, Dan had a thriving career in advertising—he'd won a Clio and a One Show Award—and I, on the other hand, had an eight-year-old Subaru burning oil every time it idled.

I comforted myself with denial and self-delusion. I told myself that this was a phase, a lark, a quick shot and then grow-up time. It's impossible to fail at something to which you've applied the most desultory and disingenuous effort. The only way to avoid frostbite and altitude sickness is not to try to climb the mountain in the first place. Leaving UCLA, I went immediately from "student"—a nice, respectable status—to "aspirant," or, worse, "wanna-be." Had I thought about it at the time, *really* thought about it, right now I'd be a third-year associate at a large New York law firm, wondering if the senior partner thinks my neckties are too flashy.

FADE OUT.

Development, Heaven and Hell

FADE IN: SUMMER 1993

Comedy writers have a long-running debate, one that lasts through bottles of wine and into the early-morning hours. It is known as the Mickey Mouse Question, and it goes like this: Mickey Mouse is not a funny character. He neither tells jokes nor does anything funny, he has no point of view, no real character, and his girlfriend is an uptight bore. Bugs Bunny, on the other hand, is a brilliantly inventive comic genius, sharp-witted, physically agile, a fearless wise guy who thinks nothing of donning a dress, producing an anvil out of thin air, kissing his enemy on the lips, and in the face of death and torture calling out a cheery "What's up, Doc?" Bugs is much funnier than Mickey, no contest. Why, then, is Mickey the billionaire movie star? People don't seem to be able to get their fill of that little rat, him with his squeaky voice and gee-whiz attitude. Mickey is completely inoffensive, involved in a long-term, caring relationship, optimistic. Bugs is the opposite: he's a wild man with a raging carrot-dependency, big with the exploding props and the verbal abuse, and one of these days he's going to go over the edge. Mickey never will. He and his girlfriend will spend their days in inoffensive, unfunny bliss. But it is Bugs who makes us laugh, and isn't that, after all, enough?

Creating a television sitcom means choosing between Mickey and Bugs, between a universe of likable, not-terribly-funny people and a universe of vaguely disturbing, very funny people. Networks tend, on the whole, not to like funny characters very much. If they had their choice, every sitcom would be a family or group of Mickeys, with maybe a Bugs living next door. Writers, unfortunately, on the whole prefer a big group of Bugses with a Mickey around to say things like "What's going on here? Are you all out of your minds?"

The network likes things likable. The writer likes things funny. Sometimes—rarely—these two forces mesh, and create a funny, likable show. Sometimes—usually—the network gets in its way and another show hits the airwaves set in the Village of Happy People, where characters learn things and share and hug and make everyone sick. And sometimes—with roughly Halley's comet's frequency—something slips through the sticky machine and comes out both funny, likable, sharp, and new. *Seinfeld*, say. Or *Cheers*.

Cheers had only one guiding principle: be funny. When in doubt, be funny. Don't go too long without a laugh. The underlying philosophy of this attitude is a kind of humility: the audience, more or less, was as intelligent as we were. They had roughly the same sense of humor, had roughly the same level of cultural awareness, were as loath to be preached to as we were. As difficult as it is for a cultural elitist—a writer! an educated person!—to admit, we were no smarter than our audience. And this, I think, is what ensnared the intellectuals into the *Cheers* trap—and make no mistake, *Cheers* was an officially approved show for highbrows and smarty-pants. We lured them into the tent with intellectual references, a few Kierkegaard jokes, a pun here or there, but what kept them watching was what kept the rest of the audience watching: we did a show about a bunch of people who hung out in a bar, a guy who chases women, another guy who talks all the time, and another guy who drinks beer after beer after beer in remorseless, unmitigated monotony.

This is what Dan and I were after: something funny, something new, something Bugs-like. Since we were then—sadly, no longer—in our twenties, it made sense to create a show about people we might know, about friends we might have, and about experiences we might remember.

It was the height of the "Generation X" obsession, and though we were technically members of that benighted demographic, we knew no one with a goatee, no slacker, no plaid shirt in a bad band. The people we knew who were between twenty and thirty all had jobs and bills and unfulfilled longings. The Gen X'ers on television and in movies all seemed like they were written by middle-aged people trying desperately to be hip. They reminded us of old Bob Hope skits, when he would don a hippie wig and love beads and prance around shouting "Groovy, baby!"

CUT TO:

INT. OUR OFFICE—DAY

SFX: *Phone rings.*

> MY AGENT (OVER PHONE)
> How's development?

> ME
> It's okay. We have an idea for a show.

> MY AGENT
> Which is?

> ME
> I think we'd rather wait and clarify it a bit before we tell it.

> MY AGENT
> Are you familiar with the term *passive aggressive*? That's what I think you're being right now.

                    ME
It's just that—

                 MY AGENT
I'm not just an agent, you know. I'm a
resource.

                    ME
I know, but—

                 MY AGENT
Every other client I have tells me their
ideas. Not you two. You two have some
kind of an insane secrets club. Okay, fine.

                    ME
Look, it's not much of an idea. It's about
five guys in their twenties who share an
apartment.

                 MY AGENT
I love it. Gen X, right?

                    ME
Well, not—

                 MY AGENT
Grunge, hanging around,
environmentalism, but with an
edge. I love it.

                    ME
Actually, we're going for something
slightly more realistic.

                 MY AGENT
Like that MTV thing?

                    ME
Realer.

MY AGENT

Realer? How realer? I mean, on that MTV thing, they show kids *in the bathroom*. How much realer do you want to get?

ME

We want to do a show about what it's really like to get out of college and face the world and be broke and struggle in your job and worry about the future. We don't want to do something bubblegum nice and we don't want to do something self-consciously Generation X-y. That's just hype and media nonsense. Most people in their twenties are working at jobs, paying off student loans, just trying to face an uncertain future.

MY AGENT

News flash: that ain't funny.

ME

It could be.

MY AGENT

What's it going to be like?

ME

What do you mean, what's it going to be like? It's not going to be like anything. It's going to be like us. It's going to be like our friends.

A long pause.

ME (CONT'D)

It's going to be a cross between *Taxi* and *Bosom Buddies*.

MY AGENT
Oh. Oh! *Oh!* I get it! I love it! Put in a "nice guy" character. And make sure the rest of them are all likable.

FADE OUT.

Studio Firepower

FADE IN: SEPTEMBER 1993

Henry Kissinger, the Mike Ovitz of diplomats, once defended Richard Nixon by saying that no matter how paranoid a person becomes, it must be remembered that "even paranoids have real enemies."

In Hollywood, of course, paranoid behavior is so prevalent, so hysterical, and in the end, so justified, that it hardly needs defending. The cringing, wheedling, red-eyed panic-meister who works in the front office of a big studio is not paranoid for nothing. The reason he chain-smokes and sweats up the sheets and sees enemies around every corner plotting his departure is simple to understand: he indeed has enemies, they are in fact around every corner, and he's right, they want him out.

If he's a valuable employee, if he's respected among his peers, the trade paper *Variety* will proclaim the next day that he "ankled"—left of his own accord, negotiated his own severance package, in general, behaved like a gentleman. If not, he will be described as "axed"—studio security was called, he was escorted off the lot. In a genteel town like this one, of course, people are rarely axed. Mostly they ankle. But there is no shame in being axed, or ankling when everyone knows it was really an axing. The only shame lies in the severance package, or lack of it. Ideally, after a spectacularly unsuccessful two or three years of studio chiefing, with an after-tax loss in the hundreds of millions of dollars, after a slew of bad-to-mediocre pictures, including one or two high-profile outright bombs, a decent studio executive should expect to be axed (though reported as ankled in the trades) with a hefty multimillion-dollar settlement. Otherwise, people might say he didn't know how to do his job.

Sad to say, the television side of the business is tougher. TV is the smarter, savvier, plain-faced little sister to the feature film's glamorous, popular, slutty lap dancer. The older girl is a wild time. She's sexy and great looking—but she's a heavy spender and a little bit stupid. The younger girl wears glasses, can read a financial statement, and is Daddy's favorite. Daddy, in this tortured analogy, represents the moneybags financiers— your Bronfmans, your Redstones, your Allens—who can spot a money tree a mile away. And money isn't growing on a feature film that cost him $60 million to make and $15 million to promote. It's growing on a tree called *Baywatch* or *Home Improvement* or *Friends*. What is the Information Superhighway, after all, but better and faster TV? And what could be more primitive, more backward, more *Luddite* than turning out the lights and making shadows on a screen?

Who do *you* want to take to dinner? Don't for a minute think that the younger, plainer, smarter sister wouldn't trade it all—her smarts, her self-respect, her money—for one chance at glamour and sex. Most TV writers actually aspire to work in features for less money and almost no power. And ordinarily smart moneymen running smart companies (think Seagram, and the Japanese before them, and Credit Lyonnais before *them*, and Coca-Cola before *them*, and TransAmerica before *them*) trip over themselves to get into a business in which employees actually compete to spend money. Their money. And when these movies don't do well at the box office—or, more realistically, do well the first weekend after multimillions are spent on bus cards and billboards and radio spots and TV commercials and the *next* weekend see a 30 percent drop-off—well, what's the excuse? We didn't spend *enough*. We only dropped $15 million for promotion. We should have dumped

20, 30, hell—50. And you'll have to pay me more next time, by the way. And I want a piece of the *un*adjusted gross from dollar one. We're partners in success. In failure, go fuck yourself.

She's a bitch, the feature business.

Dan and I have a more modest ambition. All we want is one or two shows on the air. After that, we promise to take our sacks of money home.

Okay, okay. Maybe then we'll do a feature.

                                                              CUT TO:

INT. OUR OFFICE—DAY

SFX: Phone rings.

                         MY AGENT (V.O.)
          I have good news and bad news.

                              ME
          What's the bad news?

                         MY AGENT
          Don't you want to hear the good news
          first?

                              ME
          No, actually, I'd like to hear the bad news.

                         MY AGENT
          That's not healthy. You should want to
          hear the good news.

                              ME
          Okay, okay. What's the good news?

                         MY AGENT
          Sure you want to hear?

                              ME
                         (Slowly)
          Yes.

MY AGENT

The good news is that I've finally
managed to shake off this horrible cold.

ME

Uh-huh. And what's the bad news?

MY AGENT

It's not actually that bad. [My agent
mentions the name of an important
executive at our studio] is out!

ME

What?

MY AGENT

He's out. Gone.

ME

Ankled or axed?

MY AGENT

What?

ME

You know . . . like in *Variety*? Is he ankling
or has he been axed?

MY AGENT

What the hell are you talking about? What
kind of crap is that—ankled or axed? He's
been *fired*, okay? *He's out!*

ME

Hmmm.

MY AGENT

I don't think you understand the problem
here. The man who was most responsible
for bringing you to this studio, the man
you have an *important relationship* with, is

no longer there. You are under very
different auspices, my friend. It behooves
you to establish favored-nation status with
his replacement.

                    ME
Who is his replacement?

                    MY AGENT
Let me call you back.

SFX: Click. Dial tone.

                              CUT TO:

I know my agent is serious when I hear that strange, elabo-
rate, nutty diction. I am worried. This industry runs on relationships, it is true. If the guys in the front office like you, you get
extra perks: a shower in your office, say, or aggressive support
when dealing with the television networks. But when someone
new comes in, he or she brings in a new team, to whom you are
nothing but a figure on a spreadsheet, an unproductive asset
burning up overhead expenses.

The studio, though it has agreed to pay you a minimum sum
over two years, nevertheless expects you to earn that money.
And when a new guy comes in, his first priority is to solidify his
power base by (a) firing a lot of underlings and hiring new ones
and (b) making trouble for people like me who have deals that
predate his administration.

                              CUT TO:

INT. OUR OFFICE—DAY (MOMENTS LATER)

INTERCUT WITH: INT. MY AGENT'S OFFICE—
DAY

                    MY AGENT (INTO PHONE)
I know who the new person is at your
studio.

ME

Who is it?

*My agent mentions someone I've never heard of. This
isn't hard, as I've really never heard of most people who
work in this business.*

ME (CONT'D)

Who's that?

MY AGENT

Excuse me? *Hellooo?* Are you in this
business?

ME

Sorry. I've never heard of the guy.

MY AGENT

It doesn't matter. What matters is that *I*
know who he is.

ME

And do you?

MY AGENT

You're darn right I know him. *We have
a relationship.* I told you this was
good news.

CUT TO:

Armed with this good news, Dan and I are ready to approach
our newly installed studio bosses with a television series idea.
We are ready to "pitch." The way it works is this: the studio pays
us to think up an idea. We pitch the idea to the studio development people. If they like it, we then go to a television network
(for us, one network in particular; we have a *relationship* with
that one, you see). If the network likes it, we write the first, or
pilot, script. If they like the script, we cast and shoot the pilot. If
they like the pilot, we're on the air. If we're on the air, we get to

order hugely expensive lunches from hugely expensive restaurants and no one from studio accounting calls us.

It never works that way. It works this way: the studio isn't really sure about the idea, but goes along with it out of fear. The network demands changes. In one frenzied, short-tempered week, a pilot is shot. By the time the prime-time schedule is announced, sometime in May, you no longer care that the network is not selecting your show for its fall schedule.

All that matters, really, is survival: maybe your little show will be picked up by the network for its midseason schedule, as a replacement for one of the shows that the network currently professes absolute confidence in. Maybe you sell your show to another network. Or, maybe, you just take a few months off and come back fresh for midseason, or next season, or something. You have failed, but in that inexorable, peculiar, nerve-wracking Hollywood way, you have failed upward.

                                        CUT TO:

INT. OUR OFFICE-DAY

INTERCUT WITH: MY AGENT, IN A LEXUS,
DRIVING ALONG SUNSET BOULEVARD

                    MY AGENT
        I'm going over Coldwater Canyon so this
        could get scratchy.

                        ME
        Okay.

                    MY AGENT
        ... [Inaudible] ...

                        ME
        What?

                    MY AGENT
        [Inaudible] ... idea?

ME

What?

MY AGENT

[Inaudible] . . . your pitch for Chrissakes
. . . don't . . . [inaudible] . . . around, you
know?

ME

I can't understand you. Your signal is
breaking up. Why do you insist on having
important conversations on that damn
thing when you're going over the hill? I'll
be in the office all day. Call me when you
get to a real phone.

I am about to hang up when the static suddenly clears.

MY AGENT

You don't have to get so huffy.

ME

Well, I—

MY AGENT

None of my other clients yells at me, you
know.

ME

I'm sorry.

MY AGENT
(in a tiny voice)

I have feelings, too, you know.

ME

I'm sorry.

MY AGENT

Forget it! It never happened. You have a

bad, out-of-control temper. You fly into
demonic rages. *Okay.*

                    ME
But—

                MY AGENT
You're under a lot of stress. Everyone at
the studio is new, you don't know anyone
in the development office, the studio is
cutting back on their half-hour comedy
production, and I'm sure you've heard the
big rumors.

                    ME
What rumors?

                MY AGENT
You haven't heard?

                    ME
No. What's going on?

                MY AGENT
Brace yourself. [Inaudible] . . . in New
York tomorrow. Which means [inaudible]
. . . a tiny window of opportunity.
[Inaudible] . . . does not look good.

SFX: Static. Crackle. Then nothing.

                            CUT TO:

    Later that day I discover what the rumor is. The first thing I
learn is that it is not a rumor. It is the truth. Several bidders are
attempting to buy the studio where I work. I learn this at lunch
with a bunch of other writers. A discussion of the various possi-
bilities, and the future of our business, ensues.

CUT TO:

EXT. PATIO, COLUMBIA BAR & GRILL—DAY

*The Columbia Bar & Grill—or "C. Bag" as we used to
call it—is no longer in business—or, as a friend of
mine puts it, "no longer in the business of feeding people
in the Business." Its demise was a shock to most of us.
Tucked in on the corner of Sunset and Gower, it was
the TV industry's daytime commissary. On the ground
floor of the Sunset-Gower Studios, up the street from
Paramount, a ten-minute drive from Burbank—going
out to lunch to C. Bag was almost like not going out at
all, because everyone you were avoiding was there,
eating a scallop-and-arugula salad, and making the
international sign for "I'll call you": left hand in a fist
pressed against the cheek, right index finger pointing at
the designated callee.*

*Writers in development go out to lunch. Writers in pro-
duction order in. Writers in development tend to eat
together, providing all the perks of being in production
(the laughs, the gossip, the bitter complaining) without
the ghastly drawbacks (the hours, the actors, the network executives).*

*Today, we are talking about the latest takeover attempt
of our studio.*

WRITER #1
It's going to be the phone company, boys.
The phone company is going to own our
asses by Thanksgiving. I read it today in
the Calendar section of the *Times.*

WRITER #3
Which *Times?*

WRITER #1

LA.

WRITER #3

That's your problem right there. In the
New York Times, it's very clearly going to
be a consortium of cable companies.

WRITER #2

No way. That shopping-network thing.
That's what the *Journal* says.

WRITER #3

You read the *Wall Street Journal*?

WRITER #2

No. A guy on CNBC was talking about the
article.

WRITER #3

I'm telling you: a big cable company.

ME

I don't get it. Why would anyone want to
own a giant studio? How many companies
have lost their shirts in this business?

WRITER #1

You're forgetting: studios have valuable
assets.

ME

Such as?

WRITER #1

Um . . .

WRITER #2

Such as us! We're assets!

ME

We are?

WRITER #3

He's right! We are! Well, not *us personally*, but the shows we create and work on make millions and millions.

ME

So some guy is willing to spend eight *billion* dollars for *us*?

WRITER #2

Essentially.

ME

Boy. Wait till he finds out how long we take for lunch.

WRITER #4

You guys are missing the point. We as writers are under siege. The sanctity of the written word is being diminished every day. With interactive television, the art of storytelling will gradually fade away. And virtual reality will eliminate the need for any kind of writerly activity. It's scary. We're the last practitioners of our art form. We're the last artists of the written word. As keepers of the ancient troubadour's art, we should be more vigilant about the growing corporatism and coarsening of what is, in fact, the most profoundly humanistic activity ever—man's highest achievement.

ME

What's your new show about again?

                    WRITER #4
A little black boy who's adopted by an old
lady with superpowers. And who knows?
With all this upheaval, I may never see a
dime of syndication money.

                    WRITER #2
Jesus, really?

                    WRITER #4
Really.

                                        CUT TO:

Later that day, it's time for the pitch. My agent drops by the
office before the meeting, in what is billed as a casual "I-was-on-
the-lot-for-other-business-thought-I'd-drop-by" drop-by, but is, in
fact, an "I'm-coming-to-the-pitch-with-you-whether-you-like-it-or-
not" drop-by.

Our agent comes to meetings with us. At first, we thought
this was standard operating procedure, until an older, wiser,
more experienced writer took us aside and said: "You know,
having your agent come to meetings and pitches makes you
look like the two biggest *wusses* in town."

So we're trying to wean ourselves from agent-in-towism.
Today, though, is not the day to make our stand. This is our first
meeting with the new management of the studio—new, that is,
for now; the buyout still hasn't taken place, so there's a *new* new
management somewhere in the wings—and it's important that
we get them enthusiastically behind our sitcom idea.

                                        CUT TO:

EXT. STUDIO LOT—DAY

We walk with our agent across the lot to the Adminis-
tration Building.

                    MY AGENT
Be very up, okay? Really sell. Put your

brain in come-and-get-me mode. Don't just
sit there like you do in my office. Come
alive.

> MY
>
> ME

I'm not going to hop around the room and
humiliate myself.

> MY AGENT

Who's telling you to do that? Did I say do
that? I never said "hop around the room."
I said, *"Be active, move around the room,"*
is what I said.

> ME

Okay.

> MY AGENT

But hopping can be effective, since you
brought it up. It gets their attention.

> ME

Shouldn't the fact that they're paying us a
lot of money to come up with ideas be
enough? Shouldn't simple business
acumen be enough of a motivator?
They've paid us to do a job and we've done
it. Why should we have to sell ourselves?
We're already bought.

*My agent grabs my arm and pulls me away from the
Administration Building door.*

> MY AGENT
> *(to Dan)*

Let's reschedule. He's babbling.

> CUT TO:

So we reschedule. The pitch meeting is set for next week.

The studio takeover battle continues to rage. The stock has hit a high of eighty dollars per share. Whoever wins, it is clear that there will be sweeping changes at the top.

CUT TO:

INT. OUR OFFICE—DAY

SFX: Phone rings. I answer.

INTERCUT WITH: INT. MY AGENT'S OFFICE— DAY

SFX: NBC Money Wheel *on television in background.*

> MY AGENT
>
> It's "good news, bad news" time. I'll give you the bad first, because you're so pessimistic. The development guy at your studio is out.

> ME
>
> Wow.

> MY AGENT
>
> He was an idiot anyway. It's actually good that he's out. But it means that your pitch meeting is postponed until his replacement is settled.

> ME
>
> Who's the replacement?

> MY AGENT
>
> What does it matter? You don't know anyone anyway. But actually, he's a writer—a *former* writer, I should say—so you may know him. Did the pilot about the black kid and the old lady who can fly and read minds. It was a cute show. The

network just didn't buy it, though. It was too *edgy*, you know?

> ME
>
> So what's the good news?

> MY AGENT
>
> The good news is that your studio's stock just hit eighty dollars per share.

> ME
>
> Why is that good news?

> MY AGENT
>
> It's good news if you bought at twenty-five dollars.

> ME
>
> Yeah, but I didn't.

> MY AGENT
>
> Yeah, but I *did*.

FADE OUT.

Secret Agent

FADE IN: OCTOBER 1993

In Vietnam, in the summer, the heat can get so intense that in the city markets, the caged monkeys slowly go bonkers. Their tiny brains, genetically designed for a leafy jungle climate, quite literally cook in the hot city sun. As they turn alternately catatonic and mad, the monkeys begin to attack each other with tremendous violence. The few that manage to survive their time in the cages can then look forward to the relative peace and tranquility of being eaten for dinner.

Los Angeles in October is a bit like that, except for the smell. October is the month of heat waves and smog alerts and hellish, apocalyptic canyon fires. The Santa Ana winds—hot, dry desert winds that whip through the city for days on end—work their October magic. The final box-office figures for the summer movies come rolling in, and with them the ritual movie-studio firings and resignations and "seeking other creative venues" memos—something like: "It is with great regret that I accept the resignation of Hapless Studio Executive. In his 18 months with our studio, Hapless has made invaluable contributions and will be missed. We wish him great success as he seeks other creative venues. Signed, Triumphant Ruthless Shark."

Just as the tension eases on the feature-film side of the studio lot, it heats up considerably on the television side. About the third week in September, the television networks premiere their fall schedules, in what must rate as one of the finest displays of corporate incompetence in the world. By the end of October, most of them have failed, and the ones that had been highly touted as surefire hits—pegged by Madison Avenue advertising agencies and network bosses as absolutely-no-doubt-about-it-go-ahead-and-spend-the-money hits—well, those are dead by October 1.

Happily, we're not on the air. For the first time in our short careers, the fall television schedules are an abstraction, and we view them with a certain disinterested gaze.

It's a curious attitude switch: with a show on the air, you become a tireless handicapper—"If they move *The Nanny* to Wednesday, and shift us to Monday, we get the football lead-in, which is our demo . . . look at our numbers in Minneapolis!"—and an even more desperate excuse-monger—"Of *course* we dropped six points, we were up against live hurricane coverage in Dallas, and they don't promote us, and our lead-in is weak, and the numbers are wrong!"

Without, as they say in Texas, "a dog in the fight," the whole business seems like an interesting chess game. Kind of like semiretirement.

Sadly, it's a short-lived retirement. By mid-October, we've pitched our series idea to the studio, and are polishing up the concept before we take it to the network, billed in a way guaranteed to create really rotten karma: "The guys who ran *Cheers* have an idea for a new show!"

INT. OUR OFFICE—DAY

We're sitting in the large room of our bungalow on the lot. On the wall, a blank greaseboard, save for one word written in large green letters: "Characters??"
SFX: Phone rings.

INTERCUT WITH: EXT. LAX AIRPORT—DAY

My agent races through the terminal, on a cellular phone.

MY AGENT

How's the thinking coming along?

ME

Fine, I guess. A little slow, maybe.

MY AGENT

Slow? Slow? Who cares how long it takes?
Listen, don't let them rush you. You're
creative. You need time. Your idea is solid,
and terrific, and funny, and you shouldn't
worry about some studio geek's idea of a
schedule, okay? *Okay?*

ME

Okay.

MY AGENT

I'm going to be out of town for a week
or so.

ME

Oh. Okay. What if we go to the network
before you get back?

MY AGENT

Won't happen.

ME

How do you know?

MY AGENT

Because I'm going to be *out of town*. They
know that. You know that. We'll all start
talking again when I get back. *Okay?*

ME

Okay. Fine. Maybe I'll get out of town for
a week or so too.

                    MY AGENT
        Forget about it. You should be thinking
        about what you're going to do if the
        network passes on your idea. I mean, let's
        be honest here: it's a flimsy premise and a
        long shot at best.

                        ME
        Wha—

                    MY AGENT
        No time to talk, tiger. They're boarding.

SFX: Static.

                FLIGHT ATTENDANT (O.S.)
        We'd like to board our first-class
        passengers to the Big Island of Hawaii—

SFX: Static. Click.

                                        CUT TO:

    Perhaps it isn't the smoggy air, or the 90 percent humidity, or
the blood-boiling temperatures that drive those monkeys to
madness and violence. Perhaps they all have agents.
    So I sit in my office, drinking from a tiny bottle of French min-
eral water, thinking about the future. The newspaper and the
trade papers have been read, lunch has been ordered and eaten,
so my plan is to do a quick bit of thinking about the future, and
then home by three or so. Another phone call, this one, happily,
not from my agent, but from a friend of mine from film school.
This friend now works for a rival agent at an extremely aggressive, extremely cutthroat young agency.

                                        CUT TO:

INT. OUR OFFICE—DAY

INTERCUT WITH:

INT. MY FRIEND'S BOSS'S OFFICE

My friend is on the speakerphone. His boss is staring at him while he's talking to me, all the while fiddling with two steel balls.

MY FRIEND
How's it going?

ME
Fine. As a matter of fact—

MY FRIEND
Look, I'll cut to the chase here. I know you're busy. Are you happy with your agent?

ME
That's an awfully complicated question.

MY FRIEND
Because I'll be honest with you, my boss would really like to sign you and Dan. I mean, really. Really really really. How about breakfast tomorrow at nine. No, ten. Ten. The Four Seasons at ten. Okay?

ME
Um . . .

MY FRIEND
C'mon! You guys have a big future! The whole town is talking about your new series idea! Personally, I *love* it. I mean *love*, like I'm *in love with it.*

I glance up at the greaseboard. Beneath "Characters??" is scrawled: "Story??"

ME
What, specifically, do you love about it?

                    MY FRIEND
The milieu.

                      ME
The milieu. Hmmmm.

                    MY FRIEND
C'mon! Have breakfast! (in a low voice)
It'll really raise my stock around here . . .
okay? Be a pal. . . .

                      ME
Well, you see—

                    MY FRIEND
Perfect. See you there.

*This time no click, no dial tone. Instead, I hear my
friend shouting to his secretary to get the head of one of
the networks on the line:*

                MY FRIEND (CONT'D)
Maris, get me Jeff Sagan—

SFX: Now I hear the click. Now the dial tone.

                                        CUT TO:

   My friend has done this purposely to impress me. He wants me
to know that he calls people like Jeff Sagansky—then the head of
CBS—on the telephone. What he doesn't realize is that to me, and
to almost every other writer in television, talking to network presidents on the telephone more often than not comes under the cate-
gory of Grim Duty, not Bit of Sunshine in a Dark World.
   But because I am weak and easily pushed around, I arrive at
the Four Seasons promptly at ten, convinced that I'm about to
meet with an agent I have no intention of signing with, and to eat
a breakfast I have no intention of paying for. On the grounds that
he gets pushed around by his own friends, and so has no intention of being pushed around by mine, Dan skips the breakfast.

To be honest, a part of me is curious. And an even bigger part of me is willing to entertain the possibility of switching agents. The fellow I'm about to meet is a dynamic powerhouse. He's famous for his excellent client list—as is my agent—and for his ability to get the very best deal for his clients—as is my agent. He's also deferential, quiet, and a good listener. My agent falls somewhat short on those particular points.

The Four Seasons Hotel in Beverly Hills is the only place in town to have a private meal that is nonetheless seen and noted by everyone in town. It's the home of the breakfast meeting. If my agent were not out of town, I would have insisted that we meet somewhere else. Meeting another agent for breakfast at the Four Seasons is as discreet as, well, meeting another woman for breakfast at the Four Seasons. It implies a certain willingness to go public, an indifferent attitude.

CUT TO:

INT. FOUR SEASONS HOTEL—DAY

I walk in, give my name to the hostess, grab a copy of Variety *from the stack by the phone, and in a flash, I'm ushered to my friend's table, beneath one of the brightest lights in the place.*

The table is one of three that is raised on a small platform. It is the center table, flanked by two enormous flowerpots. It is impossible not to notice us. It is impossible not to know what is going on: two men in suits plying another man in jeans and a polo shirt with orange juice and coffee. Suddenly, as I ascend the platform and take my place under the searchlight, I know what it feels like to cheat on one's spouse. Except in this case, the best I'm going to get out of the bargain is breakfast.

Handshakes all around. Some brief, insincere flattery. Coffee is poured. I order the "Alternative Cuisine" breakfast, which is, essentially, a bowl of cereal and a fat-free muffin. It will cost this agent and his agency roughly seventeen dollars.

My friend says nothing. He stares at me robotically throughout the following.

> AGENT
> I hear you're not happy with your agent?

> ME
> Well, that's not entirely true.

> AGENT
> Of course it isn't. But you're not sure you're getting the best career advice, right?

> ME
> Well, maybe.

> AGENT
> Of course well maybe. Let me be totally honest with you. You're not. No well. No maybe. Even if I wasn't interested in signing you—which I am
> *(laughs)*
> —even if I wasn't even in the agency business—which I am
> *(laughs again)*—
> I'd tell you to look elsewhere. I would. Really. I'm not even lying to you.

I look over at my friend, who is busily spreading pear butter on a carrot muffin. He spreads the pear butter thickly, and with great intensity, on one half of the muffin, then on the other. Then he places both halves on his bread plate. Then his boss, the agent, picks up a half and takes a big bite.

(mouth full)

Let me tell you something about myself. I
have no life. I have no wife. I have no
girlfriend. I go home at eleven, sometimes
twelve o'clock, and I'm up by six. What do
I do with all my time? What do I do? *I
serve my clients. That's what I do.* I'm not
an agent agent. It's not my job. *It's my
state of being.* Okay?

*He pops the other half into his mouth and chews at me.
I'm very frightened. All of a sudden I realize that of our
little breakfast party, this agent is the youngest one present. I am twenty-eight years old, and I'm having breakfast with a man who is younger than I, has his muffins
buttered and dressed by an underling, who has no life
and is proud of it, and who, if he gets his way, will be
calling me at least once a week. No, I think to myself,
I'd rather stick with the devil I know. I'll take the quick
shifts of opinion, the endless vacations, the indifference,
the sometimes incoherent conversations. My agent may
be irritating, but compared to the man who's buying me
breakfast, I have it easy.*

CUT TO:

Later, back at the office, the agent calls. I am sitting in my
office with a few other writers, and when my secretary tells me
who is on the phone, I suddenly have the urge to pick up the
phone and whisper urgently, "Darling, I told you never to call
me here. . . ."

CUT TO:

INT. MY OFFICE—DAY

The agent calls. I put him on the speakerphone.

> AGENT (O.S.)
> How'd I do? Have you talked about it with
> Dan? Are we in bed together?

An unfortunate turn of phrase, but very common in Hollywood. Sexual metaphors are rampant in business discussions, mostly due to the high probability that one party is about to be screwed.

> ME
> You know what? Breakfast was great and I
> liked what you had to say, but to tell you
> the truth, I'm happy where I am. Thanks.

A long silence.

> AGENT
> Okay. Fine. You're making a big, dumb
> mistake. A huge career-killing mistake.
> But I respect you for it. I respect your
> loyalty. Give me a call if you change
> your mind.

> ME
> I will. Thanks.

But before I can say good-bye:

> AGENT
> Noreen, get me Warren Littlefie—

SFX: Click. Dial tone.

CUT TO:

The great thing about flattery is how flattering it is. Just knowing that someone as young and sharklike as that agent wants to sign us is a tremendous energy boost. We work feverishly for several more days, convinced, beyond all reason, that the series idea we have yet to announce, involving characters we have yet to settle on, following a story we have yet to conceive, is nevertheless the talk of the town.

We are hot, we tell each other. We are sought after, we say. Our profile is rising. Our days as "the guys who run *Cheers*" are over; we're "industry professionals" now. Players. And if it took a little disloyalty to find out, well, it's a small price to pay.

CUT TO:

INT. OUR OFFICE—DAY

> MY AGENT
> Hi. Back again.

> ME
> How was your vacation?

> MY AGENT
> Wonderful. And how was *your* week?

> ME
> *(Guilty, acting cool)*
> What? What do you mean? What does that mean?

> MY AGENT
> Nothing. Just a question.

Somebody told. Somebody saw us eating at the altar in the Four Seasons. I'm dead. Dead.

> MY AGENT (CONT'D)
> You sound nervous.

> ME
> Well . . . I'm a little . . . tired.

> MY AGENT
> From what?

ME
(*Defensive, hysterical*)
From thinking, okay? From thinking
about the new show! What if nobody
wants it?

MY AGENT
What are you talking about? Everyone
loves the concept.

ME
What?

MY AGENT
I called the network driving back from the
airport yesterday. Gave them a "heads
up." They *love* the milieu. By the way, is
the messenger there?

ME
What messenger?

*My secretary tells me that the messenger is indeed there,
as if by cue, with a large envelope. I open up the envelope and a document tumbles out, spiked by red plastic
tabs, indicating the places for me to sign and initial.*

ME (CONT'D)
The guy just got here. What's this?

MY AGENT
Sign and give it back to him to bring back
to me.

ME
What is it?

MY AGENT
Oh, it's the standard agency renewal
contract. You know, what you signed

when I took you on as a client? When you
were a starving film student? When I took
a chance on you and staked my reputation
on you? Remember? It expires officially
next month, but I thought, hell, why not
get a jump on things. So sign. *Now.*

I sign.

                    MY AGENT (CONT'D)
Let's meet. Catch up. Talk. Whatever.

                         ME
Okay. Breakfast?

                    MY AGENT
No. Dinner. Nothing gets accomplished
over breakfast. Right?

                         ME
Right.

                    MY AGENT
                    (Cheery)
Right. See you tonight.

                         ME
Tonight? I can't—

                    MY AGENT
Great!

                         ME
But—

                    MY AGENT
Jason, get me Jeffrey Katz—

SFX: Click. Dial tone.

                              FADE OUT.

HIPE

FADE IN: JANUARY 1994

The main reason that television sitcoms are so bad is that too many educated people are involved in creating them. The television development process works like this: writer comes up with idea; writer pitches idea to studio; studio "gives notes"—that is, suggestions for changes and additions; writer and studio then go to network to pitch idea; network then either has no interest, or does, in which case it "gives notes"; writer and studio come back to network with refined idea, incorporating network notes; network then either has interest and "green-lights" the project, in which case writer begins writing script, or network loses interest and tries, instead, to interest writer in a show that the head of the network came up with about a talking dog who can only be heard by a mildly retarded little girl.

The intensity of the network's enthusiasm depends upon the pitch. And the pitch, foolishly enough, depends on the writer.

The dirty little secret of the entertainment industry is that everyone in it is a salesman. A nicely dressed salesman, sure, but beneath the Armani and the Revos flutter-beats the heart of a sample-case-lugging, family-neglecting, wife-cheating, just-trying-to-catch-a-dime salesman. Think Willy Loman with a cell phone.

Out here, we call it a "pitch." Anywhere else, they'd call it what it really is: "a sales call."

BEGIN FLASHBACK SEQUENCE

INT. NETWORK COMMISSARY—DAY

Early morning. For some reason, Dan and I have been enlisted by the studio (and our agent) to pitch a Cheers *spin-off. It's a long, long shot, as everyone (except us) knows, but the current studio head is a legendary salesman, and has a compulsive need to sell TV shows twenty-four hours a day.*

The news that Cheers *would not return for a twelfth season was still fresh. The studio and our agent had cajoled us into coming up with a quasi-spin-off idea for one of the cast members (no, not Kelsey Grammer of* Frasier, *sad to say) who had shown only the barest glimmer of desultory interest in the series. But, good boys, we think up a series idea and head to the network. It is our first pitch. It is, truth be told, our first meeting with anyone from the network. Although we have been writing and producing* Cheers *for two years, we're still very new to the business, still the "boys."*

The studio executive arrives late. He hustles in.

STUDIO EXEC
Ready?

MY AGENT
Of course they're ready! Of course!

We head up to the network president's office.

STUDIO EXEC
What are we pitching, again?

ME
Um . . . a *Cheers* spin-off.

STUDIO EXEC

We are? Great, great.

We stride down the hall to the door.

STUDIO EXEC (CONT'D)

Top-line me.

He keeps charging down the hall. Stops at the network president's door.

ME

You don't know what the show is about?
You didn't read the material we sent over?

STUDIO EXEC

Nope.

ME

Um . . . okay, the show is about—

STUDIO EXEC

Too late!

He hustles into the office, and is glad-handing the gathering like a city councilman up for reelection. The office is packed: me, Dan, my agent, the studio exec, the network president, the network vice president, the network's other vice president, the network head of "current comedy," and someone else who I still—almost four years later—cannot identify with any certainty.

STUDIO EXEC (CONT'D)

We've got the funniest goddamn idea I've
ever heard in *my life*! *In my whole fucking
life*! And I'll be totally honest with you
guys—right here, right now—if you don't
want it, you're fucking nuts, *fucking
nuts*!—but fine, okay, I've got two other

---

buyers who *cannot wait to get into business with these two guys!*

Dramatic pause. He nods at my partner, Dan.

> STUDIO EXEC (CONT'D)
> Rob—

He nods at me.

> STUDIO EXEC (CONT'D)
> —and Dan—they *know how to do a television show.*

Another pause. I do not know it yet, but for years to come, the network president will get me and Dan mixed up.

> STUDIO EXEC (CONT'D)
> Hit it.

And I begin to pitch our idea. My agent, for the first time, is silent. In one feverish thirty-minute blast, Dan and I outline the characters, the story of the first episode, and sketch out a few more possible story ideas.

The studio executive laughs the loudest, nudges the network president a few times, as if to say: "See? aren't my boys good?" and generally behaves like a nervous host. But his eyes are glassy and out of focus. His laughter, while loud, is sometimes strangely out of sync with the pitch.

We finish to general laughter. A pause.

> STUDIO EXEC (CONT'D)
> (slowly, with passion)
> This is a show about *people with dreams. . . .*

INT. NETWORK OFFICES HALLWAY—LATER

The pitch has gone well. My knees are still wobbly. I didn't realize how nervous I was until I stood up from the couch and felt cold sweat patches on the backs of my knees and saw the twisted shreds of the note pages in my hands.

                    ME
    How'd we do?

                STUDIO EXEC
    We made a sale, kiddo.

                    ME
    Great!

                STUDIO EXEC
    What's the show about, again?

                                    CUT TO:

A few weeks later, the show and the pilot faded away. The star lost interest, we were tied up wrapping the last few episodes of *Cheers*, the heat on the idea steamed away and evaporated.

                                    CUT TO:

INT. OUR OFFICE—DAY

SFX: Phone call.

                MY AGENT
    The pilot went away.

                    ME
    What?

                MY AGENT
    Your pilot. It *went away*.

ME

Went away where?

MY AGENT

Who knows where. It just up and went.

ME

Well, can we send somebody after it to grab it and bring it back?

MY AGENT

What are you talking about?

ME

What are *you* talking about?

MY AGENT

I'm talking about the show you pitched. Since the actor passed on it, it's a dead project. The good news is that the studio guy loved the idea. I mean he *loved* it.

ME

What, specifically, did he love about it?

MY AGENT

The milieu.

ME

He loved the milieu?

MY AGENT

He *freaked* for the milieu.

ME

Yeah, but it's a dead issue. It was a waste of time.

MY AGENT

How so?

ME

Well, we didn't sell the pilot. We went
there to sell a series and we didn't sell it.

MY AGENT

Is that what you think? That you went
there to sell a series?

ME

Didn't we?

MY AGENT

Of course not. You're never selling the
series. You're never selling the pilot.
You're never selling the idea.

ME

Then what *are* we selling?

MY AGENT

Yourselves, shitbird! You're selling
yourselves. You're saying, "Hey, we're
players in the big game, get in business
with us!"

ME

And this means . . . what, exactly?

MY AGENT

It means four things. It means the
network likes you, which means the
studio likes you. It means one day one
way you'll have a show on the air. And it
means that I am a very, very good agent.

ME
(counting)

That's three things.

MY AGENT
My being a good agent counts as two
things.

ME
But—

MY AGENT
Good-bye! And *you're welcome.* . . .

CUT TO:

END FLASHBACK SEQUENCE

Nine months later, we pitched our second series to the network. By this time, we were grizzled veterans. The studio executive had left (ankled, axed, whatever) a few months before,
but his replacement drove the same make and model car (Mer-
cedes SE something) walked the same wearying walk into the
network commissary, turned on the same I'm-dancing-as-fast-as-
I-can charm the minute we hit the room. The only real difference came at the end of the pitch, while we were walking down
the hall. I asked him how we did. Instead of a cheerful "We
made a sale, kiddo!" came a bleaker, more realistic "How the
hell should I know? This fucking business is *crazy.*"

As it turned out, we made a sale, kiddo. We now had a pilot
script in development. Which means everyone pitches in to turn
a fairly simple idea and a fairly humorous little script into a perfect vehicle for Mickey Mouse.

People in this business love their souped-up vocabulary: we
"green-light" things, and dump things in "turnaround" and
"negative pickup" and "pitch" and make "preemptive strikes."
And we love our creative talk too: we like lots of "character con-
flict" and "story integrity" and "deeply humanistic values." So
when the studio and network executives give notes to a writer,
the language can be dizzying.

CUT TO:

INT. NETWORK EXEC'S OFFICE—DAY

Our first note session.

>   NETWORK EXEC #1
> Can we platform some of the characters in
> a slightly better way?

>   NETWORK EXEC #2
> Can one of them cry? Or be quirky?

>   NETWORK EXEC #1
> I *love* quirky.

>   NETWORK EXEC #3
> These characters should love each other.
> And we should see them loving each
> other.

>   NETWORK EXEC #2
> A quirky love.

>   NETWORK EXEC #1
> I *love* a quirky love.

>   NETWORK EXEC #4
> Don't worry so much about the jokes.

>   NETWORK EXEC #1
> It doesn't have to be funny. It'd be great if
> it was funny, but it doesn't have to be
> funny.

>   NETWORK EXEC #4
> Make it humorous.

>   NETWORK EXEC #2
> Or quirky.

NETWORK EXEC #1
Think about it this way. If *Cheers* was a
place "everybody knows your name" then
your show should be a place where . . . ?

NETWORK EXEC #2
Where . . . what?

NETWORK EXEC #1
Do you see the problem?

CUT TO:

We don't see the problem, but we say we do, make a few
scribbles, and get to work on the script.

CUT TO:

INT. MY BEDROOM—7:30 a.m.

SFX: Phone rings.
I struggle to the phone, answer it.

ME
Hello?

SFX: Mariachi music over phone.

MY AGENT
Hi!

ME
Yeah, hi.

MY AGENT
Did I wake you?

ME
Not yet.

MY AGENT
Here's the thing. They want the script
soon. They want it Friday.

                              ME
                        (wide awake)
                    Friday? This Friday?

                          MY AGENT
                    Actually, *last* Friday.

                              ME
                    Impossible.

                          MY AGENT
                    Of course it's impossible. What are you? A
                    time-traveler?

                              ME
                    No. I mean this Friday is impossible. And
                    next Friday is impossible too. We need   :
                    two weeks, at least. Tell them two weeks.

                          MY AGENT
                    I can't do that. Number one, I'm on
                    vacation. I'm calling you from Cozumel.
                    And (B) I already told them they could
                    have it Friday.

                              ME
                    What?

                          MY AGENT
                    I gotta go. We're all going snorkeling
                    before they start the lunch buffet.

                                               CUT TO:

    This is an example of what I call the "Hollywood Inversion
Principle of Economics." The HIPE, as it will come to be known,
postulates that every commonly understood, standard business
practice of the outside world has its counterpart in the entertainment industry. Only it's backward. In the outside world, for
instance, a corporation's financial health is determined by,

among other things, its annual net profit statement. In Hollywood, as the HIPE predicts, it is determined by the *gross* profit statement. The difference should be clear even to people like me, who bluffed their way through one low-level economics course. Gross profit is meaningless. After the payroll is met, and taxes paid, and the producer gets his 20 percent, and the actors their 15 percent, and the director his 16.7 percent, and the budget overruns are paid for, and the prints and advertising . . . well, you can start to see why the Japanese tried so recently to sell Columbia and Universal studios back to the gypsies who sold it to them in the first place.

What no one realizes—or, more accurately, no one except those *selling a studio or assisting in the selling of a studio* realizes—is that the economics of film production are designed to make individuals very rich. Shareholders are entirely out of the picture. Many of them, for some reason, are dizzied by the HIPE. The near-term return on any investment—feature film, TV show, CD-ROM thing—is entirely spoken for by the savvy participants. The studio—and its hapless, sorry-they-ever-heard-of-Herb-Allen owners—must play the long, long game, hoping that the copyright value of a *Forrest Gump* or a *Batman Forever* pays off. Or that the television show that they deficit-finance at a couple of hundred thousand dollars a throw will, eventually, pay off in reruns. There's an awful lot of hoping in this business.

Another example of HIPE is in the sheer number of agents, studio executives, network programmers, attorneys, and assorted assistants-to and associates-of who are completely at the mercy of the timetable of the lazy, good-for-nothing, shiftless writer. In the outside world, lawyers and executives are the "go slow" guys, the bottlenecks in neckties. "Don't do anything until we hear from the lawyers," they say. "I want my team of executives to take a look at this," we hear.

In Hollywood, though, everything can happen in an instant except the one thing that can't—the writing. All the Mike Ovitzes and the Barry Dillers in the world can't change this essential bedrock truth: writers like to sleep late, they like to read the newspaper slowly, they like to have long lunches, and they hate to write.

CUT TO:

INT. OUR OFFICE—DAY

I am watching cartoons on the TV that the studio foolishly provided. Dan is doing his taxes.
SFX: Phone rings.
I press the mute button on the remote control.

STUDIO EXEC

Hi.

ME

Hi.

Pause. Bugs Bunny and Daffy Duck are fighting over whether it's rabbit season or duck season.

STUDIO EXEC

How's it going? Are you having fun?

ME

No.

Pause. Bugs has produced a calendar and is wearing a dress.

STUDIO EXEC

So we're thinking . . . what? . . . Script on Friday, say? Around Friday? Morning?

ME

I don't think so.

Pause. Daffy has a gun.

STUDIO EXEC

Gee, we really need that script.

ME

We're working on it, okay? They don't
appear by magic, you know. We're making
adjustments, we're trimming, we're
tweaking. *Stop nagging us!*

*I click off the mute button and hang up. But maybe I'm
too slow, and maybe the sound from the TV comes
up before the receiver goes down, and maybe right
before he hears a dial tone, the studio executive hears
Bugs Bunny screaming, "Oh, Mr. Fudd, you're sooo
handsome!"*

*I've surprised myself: a few months ago, I wouldn't have
dreamed of refusing a studio request. I have indeed
graduated from "one of the boys who runs* Cheers." *I
am now "Jesus Christ what happened to* him? *He used
to be so* nice."

CUT TO:

There's nothing to do but go to lunch, which poses a conun-
drum. Wherever we go, we're bound by the dictates of karmic
bad luck to run into our Studio Executive. How, in good con-
science, can we claim to be both feverishly toiling on our script
and lingering over a radicchio-and-braised-scallop salad? We
solve this problem by bringing along an empty notebook and an
old, inkless pen. If caught, we'll wave the executive away with a
frown as our pen scratches across the paper leaving no mark.
We reflect happily that this technique will also serve to establish
our lunches, especially the expensive ones, as working lunches,
and therefore fully tax-deductible.

CUT TO:

INT. OUR OFFICE—DAY

4:00 p.m. I am smoking a cigar and finishing a small whiskey from a bottle I keep around the office for emergencies.
SFX: Phone rings.

MY AGENT
I hear you yelled at a studio exec.

ME
I didn't yell.

MY AGENT
I didn't say you did.

ME
Yes you did.

MY AGENT
You're getting defensive.

ME
Yeah, but—

MY AGENT
What is this? A "gotcha" conversation?
Are we playing "gotcha"? Well, fine, but I
can play with the best of them, okay?

Pause. I pour myself another Scotch.

ME
Okay, okay. I yelled.

MY AGENT
Good for you. Bust his chops a little. If
they push and you roll, then the next time
they just push harder. You want me to call
him and scream a little?

                              ME
         No, no. You're on vacation. I can
         handle this.

                         MY AGENT
         Because it's no trouble.

                              ME
         Really. No.

Pause.

                         MY AGENT
         Please?

                              ME
         If you really want to.

                         MY AGENT
         It's raining down here and I'm going out
         of my tree.

                                        CUT TO:

BEGIN MONTAGE

1. A CLOCK—
         hands spinning around the face, time
         passing.

2. A SPINACH-AND-POACHED-SALMON SALAD—
         disappearing in time-lapse photography.

3. A COMPUTER SCREEN—
         filling up with dialogue in screen format.

4. ANOTHER SALAD—

5. A CIGAR, BURNING—

6. THE CLOCK—
         spinning . . .

7. AN HP LASERJET PRINTER—
    spitting out pages.

END MONTAGE

                                DISSOLVE TO:

INT. OUR OFFICE—DAY

SFX: Phone rings.

INTERCUT WITH:

INT. OUR AGENT'S OFFICE—DAY

Our script is lying open on our agent's desk.

                MY AGENT
    I love it. It's hysterical. It's brilliant. It's
    perfect.

                ME
    I'm glad to hear it.

                MY AGENT
    Besides, you'll punch it up.

                ME
    What?

                MY AGENT
    It's a first draft. First drafts are first drafts.
    The studio will have notes. The network
    will have notes. *I* have notes.

                ME
    I thought you said it was perfect.

                MY AGENT
    Nothing is perfect.

                ME
    But you said—

MY AGENT

What? "Gotcha" again?

ME

Well, what should we do? Should we send
it to the studio now?

MY AGENT

Don't you want to hear my notes?

ME

Not really.

Pause.

MY AGENT

You're being passive-aggressive.

ME

I'm sorry. I'm trying to be aggressive-
aggressive.

MY AGENT

Funny. Look, it's reality time, okay?
Everyone is going to have notes. They're
all going to want changes. Some changes
you make. Some you fight.

ME

Uh-huh.

MY AGENT

Mine you make.

ME

And theirs?

MY AGENT

You make theirs too.

ME

Whose do I fight?

> MY AGENT
>
> How they hell should I know? I don't have
> a crystal ball.

> ME
>
> But if I roll over every time they push,
> don't they just push harder next time?

> MY AGENT
>
> Yeah. And next time you just roll harder.
> It's like that Frank Sinatra song: "I Did It
> Their Way."

> ME
>
> That's not—

> MY AGENT
>
> I don't want to have this conversation.

CUT TO:

The next day, I read in *Variety* that superagent Swifty Lazar died. I never met Swifty, but I always admired his huge black spectacles. Perched on his bald head, which itself was perched on his tiny, round frame, the glasses made him look like a huge, jovial insect. Lazar's nickname was Swifty, but people who knew him well always called him Irving—another example of HIPE: having a nickname that's used only by people who don't know you.

Throughout the following days, Lazar's friends and clients (and, astonishingly, these groups intersected) took out advertisements in the trades to eulogize their friend, and to advertise their grief, and also, I suppose, to make it clear that they were all now seeking representation. I wonder if I will ever be in the position to eulogize my agent in the pages of *Variety*. Lazar died well into his eighties. My agent is fairly young. I am reaching for the bottle of whiskey when the phone rings.

It's the network. They have some notes. I keep the bottle handy.

FADE OUT.

Eye Candy

FADE IN: FEBRUARY/MARCH 1994

Americans have their own version of the traditional English Irish joke—that is, a joke that takes as its premise the intellectual inferiority of a different and unsuspecting nationality. Here in the United States, we have the Polish joke, and one of the more popular examples in Hollywood goes as follows: Did you hear about the Polish actress who came to Hollywood? She slept with a writer. The idea being that anyone who sleeps with a Hollywood writer in the hopes of advancing her (or his—this is a multicultural, pansexual community, after all) career has gravely, gravely misapprehended the situation.

For the most part, of course, this is an accurate assumption. Being a writer is a little bit like being a shepherd: it's quaint, people envy the solitude, but everyone knows the real money is in synthetic fibers.

In the television business, the reverse is true. Writers have a great deal of power when compared to their colleagues in the feature film business. More often than not, the television writer is what Industry contracts define as a hyphenate: a writer-producer, say, or a writer-director. This explains why some of the best, most affecting and artful comedy and drama in the United States today can be found on television. It also explains why so much on TV is such shit.

Power is not precisely accurate. Onerous and Humiliating

Duties is a better term. For though the feature film writer is cut off from the process of casting, shooting, scoring, and editing, he is usually too busy relaxing in Hawaii to care. The television hyphenate, though technically in charge of the entire production, must simper and beg and bootlick throughout the process.

The money trail, as always, tells the true story. A writer allies with a studio and together they approach a network with a proposed television show. The network is playing a short-term strategy: it makes its money by selling prime-time advertising space to national advertisers. It merely rents—or licenses, to use the Industry term—the show for two broadcasts, one first-run and one rerun. After it runs an episode of a series twice, the episode reverts back to the original owners, the studio, who are playing a long-term strategy. They need to assemble five years' worth of a series (usually one hundred episodes or so) in order to license them in bulk to the hundreds of affiliate and independent television stations all over the country who need programming for the off-hours, and non-prime-time spots on their schedules. The goal, then, is to *get on the air at all costs.* If the network puts your show on its schedule, and the show lasts four years (or one hundred episodes, whichever comes first) then the future is written on a million check stubs. A thousand roses bloom on your ranch in Montecito.

This system—a kind of nutty "lend-lease"—is fast disappearing. For years, the networks were prohibited from owning the "back end" rights to the television shows they broadcast. The Financial Interest and Syndication Rules—what we jauntily call "Fin-Syn"—were essentially antitrust rules designed to keep the networks from acquiring too much control over the nation's airwaves. With the advent of cable, and a corresponding decline in network viewer share, the rules were dropped.

In the meantime, though, the major studios had grown a pretty healthy money tree in TV show reruns. But to build up enough episodes for syndication (remember: magic number one hundred) they need access to the airwaves. Why, though, would a network, now unshackled from Fin-Syn restrictions and in the 100 percent–ownership TV production business, buy a show from an outside supplier? Why make someone else rich?

To protect themselves from being shut out of the big game, the big studios have been slowly getting into the network-ownership business. That, along with the cable channels, has trebled the number of TV show buyers. Good news for the writer in the near term: more buyers, more money, more places to sell a series; bad news for the long term: fewer independent stations buying reruns, a syndication glut, constant shuffling and tumult.

If at this point the reader is thoroughly confused, the reader must not, under any circumstances, quit his day job. If, perversely, the reader readily grasps the above concepts, the reader is encouraged to come to Hollywood to seek his fortune. If the reader is thoroughly confused, but is nonetheless intent on coming to Hollywood to seek his fortune, the reader is not a reader, he is a writer.

The writer's part in this pageant is crucial: he has to do all the work. He has to think up the show and sell the pilot and cast the episode and rewrite the script and edit the picture and, if lucky, produce the series, which airs on the network that some mogul wants to buy. He has to do this while surrounded by people—studio guys, agent guys, network guys—whose job, essentially, is to *watch* him do his job.

INT. OUR OFFICE—DAY

SFX: Phone rings.

MY AGENT

Are you excited?

ME

About what?

MY AGENT

Always so dour. Always immediately
negative. Why is that? I wonder. I meant

about your pilot. Are you excited about
your pilot?

ME
I guess. It's a lot of work, though.

MY AGENT
Of course it's a lot of work. That's the
problem with your generation. No work
ethic. I'll be at lunch until four or so. Try
to cheer up. Before I go, I just had a
brainstorm for your cast: Hugh Grant.

*N.B. This was way, way before Hugh Grant's rise, fall,
and rise again.*

ME
Hugh Grant?

MY AGENT
You know the guy. From *The Wedding
Funeral*?

ME
I don't think he'll do a series. He's a movie
star now. And besides, isn't he English?

MY AGENT
Why don't you ever see the good in
people?

DISSOLVE TO:

INT. OUR OFFICE—LATER

*We are in the midst of casting our pilot. Dan and I are
attempting to create an ensemble of young, comically
nimble actors. The network, meddlesome as always,
wants us to create an ensemble of young, comically
nimble actors who look terrific in bathing suits.
SFX: Phone rings.*

INTERCUT WITH:

INT. RANGE ROVER—DAY

The network executive is driving along San Vicente Boulevard.

> NETWORK EXEC
>
> Are you excited?

> ME
>
> About what?

> NETWORK EXEC
> *(laughing)*
> You writers! Always so sarcastic.

A long pause.

> NETWORK EXEC (CONT'D)
> Here's why I'm calling. I'm wondering if
> you've looked at [mentions the name of a
> young actor] for your show.

> ME
>
> Yeah, we looked at him.

> NETWORK EXEC
> Isn't he terrific? Isn't he the funniest?
> Don't you just want to eat him up?

Another long pause.

> ME
>
> To tell you the truth, he didn't really
> impress us.

> NETWORK EXEC
>
> I'm sorry?

ME

He had trouble pronouncing certain
words.

NETWORK EXEC

Which words?

ME

Small words. Easy words. Words, frankly,
that ordinarily don't give people trouble.

NETWORK EXEC

Well, we like him a lot over here. A lot.
And we'd like to see him in a series. Very
much. He may not be a rocket scientist,
but he's got a great look.

ME

But he's clinically illiterate.

NETWORK EXEC

And you can't work around that? Okay,
okay. You don't like him. How about
Hugh Grant?

(See note above.)

ME

Is he available?

NETWORK EXEC

Of course not. He's a movie star. I just
meant a Hugh Grant type. You know,
English. They pronounce everything so
beautifully over there. And I know what a
stickler you are about that.

DISSOLVE TO:

INT. OUR OFFICE—CONFERENCE ROOM—DAY

Later that day we see 137 young actors and actresses.
They all clutch their "sides"—theater lingo for xeroxed
excerpts of the script—in white-knuckled panic. Some
have worried the few stapled pages into a twisted twig-
looking thing, others have methodically shredded each
page (hence the term "method acting"). Many of them
have difficulty reading the words aloud. Some stumble
over syntax. Others manage to get the setup and the
punch line reversed, imbuing our simple, straightfor-
ward script with a dreamy, surreal, Luis Buñuel
quality. Mostly, though, as products of the American
education system, they answer the question: Why are
the Japanese ahead of us?

BEGIN MONTAGE

1. AN OLDER ACTRESS—

here to read for a supporting role—the
neighbor character to our main
characters, five young men who share an
apartment. It isn't a big part—a few pages,
at most—but she attacks her sides with
gusto.
A few moments after her audition:

OLDER ACTRESS
Can I say something? This writing is *deft*.
It's *highly deft* writing. That you two could
write a show about a woman who lives
next to five young men . . . what can I say?
It's something special.

2. A YOUNG ACTOR

in full grunge. He flips through the sides
quickly, runs his dirty fingers through his
greasy hair, coughs, sniffles, then:

YOUNG ACTOR
I'm gonna improv a lotta this shit, okay?

3. A YOUNG ACTRESS—
starts to read, stops, tears welling in her
eyes.

YOUNG ACTRESS
(*sobbing*)
You don't want *me*! You want somebody a
lot thinner.

4. AN OLDER ACTRESS—
here to read for the neighbor character.
She reads a bit, stops, glares at us.

OLDER ACTRESS
A woman would never say that in a million
years. You're going to change it, right?

5. SUCCESSFUL YOUNG ACTOR—
here because the network loves him and
he knows it.

SUCCESSFUL YOUNG ACTOR
My agent is begging me not to do half-
hour. He thinks I'm more of a feature
actor, y'know? But I read the script and
fell in love with it, and thought, "Hey,
maybe I *can* collaborate with these guys."
Sorry that I can't audition. You know,
formally. It diminishes me in the
marketplace.

END MONTAGE

CUT TO:

Casting, sadly, is everything. The network reserves the right
to veto any casting choice, which they exercise on an informal

basis—glaring at the actor, loudly suggesting replacements, stubbornly refusing to laugh at anything he does during run-throughs—or in a more formal way—simply demanding that he be fired before they order an episode, or worse, referring to the whole enterprise as "casting contingent."

The most unbearable part of the process is that the network is often, even mostly, right. Their casting choices are difficult to swallow precisely because they are so on-target. After all, unburdened by any serious work or responsibilities—like, say, writing the damn thing—they are free to toss around actors' names and watch lots of demo tapes. So when we troop in a motley caravan to the network's offices, bringing with us the actors we've chosen for each part—actually, *two* or more actors per role—for network casting approval, it's one of those rare moments when the network actually has something valuable to contribute.

It's galling on a biblical scale.

But it's much, much worse for the actors. By the time we drag them to the network, they've auditioned for the role no less than three times—twice for us, once for the studio—each time waiting in the waiting room with another actor who looks similar, acts similar, and who they just can't help thinking is a notch or two better-looking.

At the final network casting session, facing a grim and humorless battery of studio and network executives—sometimes a dozen or so—they often crack and deliver their lines (for the fifth time) in a totally new, totally unfunny way. It's called "unwinding at the network."

CUT TO:

INT. OUR OFFICE—DAY

SFX: Phone rings.

MY AGENT (O.S.)
Are you excited?

ME

About what?

MY AGENT

I forgot. You're playing cool. Okay, I can swing with that. I just got off the phone with the network.

ME

Oh.

MY AGENT

They're concerned.

ME

About what?

MY AGENT

They think you're going too . . . characterish . . . with your casting.

ME

What?

MY AGENT

They think you're casting ugly people.

ME

We're trying to cast good actors who can do comedy.

MY AGENT

And?

ME

And what?

MY AGENT

And who look good in their underpants.

ME

How should I know if they look good in

their underpants? Let me make this very clear: I am not going to ask someone to take off their trousers just so I can see if they look good in their underpants.

MY AGENT

So you *are* casting ugly people.

ME

We are trying to cast funny actors.

MY AGENT

Could you please tell me what's so funny about six guys who look like the Elephant Man?

ME

What?

MY AGENT

Maybe you don't understand the power structure here. The network likes young, good-looking people. America likes young, good-looking people. That's how you get on the air. That's how you stay on the air. If you've got some sicko thing for circus freaks, fine. But not on network television. My God, not after dinner. People want to see someone like Hugh Grant being funny. Why don't you cast someone like Hugh Grant?

ME

I'd love to. If you can figure out a way for us to somehow come up with six young, great-looking, funny, nimble actors who can pronounce the word "patio" then sign me up. Until then, we're stuck with thalidomide babies and bearded ladies.

CUT TO:

Unexpectedly, 10 of the 168 actors we have auditioned are both talented and suitably winsome. This enables us to go to the network with 10 choices for 6 parts, allowing the various network executives to audition each actor one more time and participate in the final decision. We could—indeed, we are legally entitled to—simply make our choices and cast our pilot as we see fit. That is, of course, the bold choice. But why be bold when one can be on the air for four years (or one hundred episodes, whichever comes first), at which point the future is written as an aimless, rich adulthood punctuated by ungrateful children?

CUT TO:

INT. MY CAR—DAY

We're driving away from the network after our final casting meeting. Remarkably, we've all agreed on our casting choices without rancor.
SFX: Car phone chirps.

INTERCUT WITH:

INT. MY AGENT'S CAR—DAY

My agent is a few cars back, heading south on the 101 Freeway.

MY AGENT
Are you disappointed?

ME
By what?

MY AGENT
No Hugh Grant.

ME
I never expected to have him in the show.

MY AGENT

Always the pessimist. Always the dark
side of life.

ME

What are you talking about? He doesn't do
series television. He was never available.
He's a movie actor.

MY AGENT

Did it ever occur to you that he may have
money trouble and may be in no position
to turn you down? Did it ever occur to you
that he may not know he's not supposed
to be interested in television? Maybe he's
ill or mentally imbalanced and that's
something you could take advantage of?

(How remarkably prescient my agent seems.)

ME

He . . . is . . . not . . . available.

MY AGENT

Maybe in a few years, then.

ME

What?

MY AGENT

He does a few bad movies, makes some
bad career moves, and before you know it,
he's ready to do a series.

ME

Hugh Grant?

MY AGENT

He's so good-looking that they'll probably

let you cast your precious circus freaks,
just for variety.

                    ME
                (sighing)
Great.

                 MY AGENT
But see him in his underpants first. You
don't want to be surprised.

                        FADE OUT.

Testing Times

FADE IN: APRIL/MAY 1994

One of the more common misperceptions of Hollywood is that it is rife with stories of overnight success. Nothing happens overnight, especially in this business. Every success, no matter how seemingly effortless, was coaxed and cajoled and, finally, extracted with tongs.

Night owls, flipping through the dozens of late-night television offerings, can sometimes spot a young Meg Ryan, say, on a really bad rerun of a really bad sitcom, *Charles in Charge*, in a really bad role. (Sample dialogue: "Oh, forget about *them*, Charles. Why don't just you and me have a little *party*!!")

It's the least one should expect from an industry whose lingo is so evocatively violent. We "shoot" things and "wrap" things and "cut" things—both "rough cuts" and the more grim "final cut"—we "pitch" things and let options "expire." The verbs are so active it's hard to believe that most of these things occur when people are sitting alone in their cars.

Exactly one year after they called "wrap" on the last episode of *Cheers*, they called "wrap" on the pilot episode of our series. The intervening months had been a long, slow fuse leading up to this particular stick of dynamite. From pitch, to notes, to script, to casting—the process is designed to drain your will and ebb your strength. Along the way, though, some surprises. Our cast, for instance. They were bright and young and very funny, of course, but they also treated us like . . . well, like, we were the bosses and we knew what we were doing. Which we were, but we didn't.

The cast of *Cheers*, as professional and pleasant as they were, knew that we were just "the boys"—caretakers of a larger enterprise. They suffered our authority; they didn't seek it out. But our cast, well, for one thing, they were *our* cast—we hired them, argued for them at the network, believed in them. And throughout the production week, after every run-through of the show, we would go back to our office and rewrite jokes, sometimes whole scenes, to tailor better our show to their talents.

A TV sitcom is filmed as if it were a stage play: in one night, in front of an audience, cameras zooming all over the place. The days leading up to "shoot night" are pretty much all the same: the actors get to the studio around nine in the morning, rehearse, sometime in the early afternoon they perform a run-through of the script for the producers (us), who then make notes, head back to their office, rewrite the script, messenger it out that night to all the actors—who tear greedily through each page, noting which actors lost lines in the rewrite, which gained them—and who then show up the next morning to rehearse the new material for the afternoon run-through . . . you can see where this is going. You do this for as many days as you can. It is nerve-shattering to the actors.

CUT TO:

INT. SOUNDSTAGE—DAY

Early morning. The actors have gathered around the table to read that day's rewrite. Although it's not usual for a producer to attend the morning reading, I do because (a) I'm a control freak and (b) I've been awake since 4:00 a.m. anyway, keyed up and nervous.

A member of our cast raises his hand.

CAST MEMBER

Does anyone mind if I take a second to
read over the script? I didn't get one last
night.

ME

You didn't?

Another cast member raises his hand.

CAST MEMBER #2

I didn't either.

CAST MEMBER #3

Me neither.

The whole cast mumbles "Me neithers" and "I didn'ts."

ME

No one got a script? I guess the
messenger service screwed up.

CAST MEMBER

I thought I was fired.

ME

What?

CAST MEMBER

I thought I was fired. I thought I gave
such a bad performance at run-through
that you guys fired me. And that's why I
didn't get a script.

ME

That's the silliest thing I've ever heard.

CAST MEMBER #2

I thought I was fired too.

CAST MEMBER #3

Me too.

---

*The rest of the cast mumbles "Me toos" and "I was sure
I was fireds."*

                    ME
          (attempting to lighten the mood)
     Hey, if we fire you, we'll send you a basket
     of those little muffins.

                CAST MEMBER
                (deadly serious)
     Oh. Okay. That's good to know.

                    ME
     I was joking. We're not firing anyone. We
     love you guys. You're terrific.

                CAST MEMBER
     Then why do you look so angry and pale
     at the run-throughs?

                    ME
     Me?

                CAST MEMBER #2
     Yeah, you.

                    ME
     That's me being *happy*. You should see
     me being *unhappy*. I'm just nervous, I
     guess.

                CAST MEMBER
     I don't know what you're nervous about.
     It's our asses they blame if it doesn't work.

Which is unfortunately untrue.

                                   CUT TO:

We shoot the pilot a few days later. The audience laughs.

_____

People seem to like the show. We quickly assemble the footage and hustle it over to the network.

May is National Broadcast Network Fall Schedule Assembly Month. The networks assemble the final versions of all of the pilots they've ordered, and begin to assemble a fall television schedule. Of the roughly one dozen pilots they order throughout the year, four or so get scheduled.

What we do during this time is what we do most of the time: we wait by the phone. The only people who call are agents, trying to angle a foot in the door to get their clients a job, should the network order our show and should we be looking to hire a writing staff. In retrospect, it's a perfect time to get out of town. Hollywood rule of thumb: When waiting, it's best to be waiting in Hawaii.

CUT TO:

INT. OUR OFFICE—DAY

SFX: Phone rings.

INTERCUT WITH:

INT. ANOTHER AGENT'S OFFICE

He is pacing his office, talking into a speakerphone. He occasionally consults an index card, on which his assistant has printed my name.

AGENT

I hear you've got a hot show!
Congratulations!

ME

Well, thanks, but you know, we've just
delivered it to the network. They haven't
bought it yet.

AGENT
Just a formality! I hear they love it! I
love it!

ME
Thanks.

AGENT
Do you know who else loves it?

ME
Who?

The agent mentions the name of one of his clients.

ME (CONT'D)
Tell him thanks.

AGENT
Tell him yourself! I'll set up a meeting!

ME
Well, you know it's a little early to be
thinking about hiring a staff. The network
hasn't bought the show.

AGENT
They will! They love it! I love it!

ME
Thanks. Again.

AGENT
Why don't I send you some of his spec
scripts! They're great!

ME
(warily)
Okay. But we're really not reading
right now.

                    AGENT
        I know! I know! But these are great!

                      ME
        Okay. But just those. Don't inundate us.

                    AGENT
        I won't! I won't! I swear to God! I'll just
        send the one spec!

                                    SMASH CUT TO:

A MESSENGER'S CLIPBOARD—

MY HAND IN FRAME, SIGNING FOR A
PACKAGE—

                                        PULL BACK:

A HUGE STACK OF SCRIPTS—

I MAKE MY WAY THROUGH THE PILE—

                                          CUT TO:

INSERT SHOT:

An agency's cover letter. It reads:

        Dear Rob:
            As per our discussion, please find enclosed
        spec scripts for the following writers . . .

*A list of seventeen names follows, each with a short
description.*

MY FINGER RUNS DOWN THE LIST—STOPPING
AT A FEW DESCRIPTIONS:
        Young, hip, dripping with smarts.
        AND: Funny to the point of hemorrhaging.
        AND: Meet him and fall in love.
        AND: Fox loves him. Won't you?

_____

This scene is repeated roughly as many times as there are lit-
erary agencies in the Los Angeles area. For five consecutive
days, the phone rings nonstop. Soon, my entire office is filled
with piles of spec scripts. I consider this a bad omen. If dozens
of agents call you to tell you that your pilot is on the short list or
a sure thing, two things are certain: you are not on the short list
and you are not a sure thing.

The studio—or, as the romantics who run things like to say,
the supplier—has meanwhile decided to market-test the
episode with a focus group. The network, of course, will test the
episode for itself, in much the same way, but the studio wants to
have its own set of data. So we troop over the hill to Burbank, to
what the romantics who run things like to call a testing facility,
and sit behind a two-way mirror to watch thirty-two demographi-
cally precise, audience-representative Americans in T-shirts
watch our show, answer questions about it, and collect twenty-
five dollars. As they file into the room, one particularly clever
young man—I shall call him Butthead—points to the mirror and
asks the group leader: "Hey. Is somebody back there, like,
watching us watch TV?" The group leader smiles and shakes his
head. "Oh no," he says, "no one is back there. No one is
watching you. Please take your seat." Butthead shrugs and sits.
A woman turns to the mirror and begins examining her teeth.

Actually, *I* am behind the mirror. Me, and about a dozen or so
people from the studio. We are watching Butthead and the
Tooth Lady and thirty of their peers watch what it has taken us
nine months and $1 million to produce. As they watch, they
manipulate a small dial attached to each chair: they twist it
clockwise if they like what they see, and anticlockwise if they
don't. A computer records their responses, collates them, and
turns the data into a line graph—or, more precisely, a two-line
graph: one line measures the men's response, the other measures the women's response. The graph is superimposed on a

tape of the show, which is playing on our side of the mirror. I am watching, essentially, an electrocardiogram of my career.

CUT TO:

INT. TESTING FACILITY—NIGHT

We're gathered in an airless, windowless, pizza-reeking room, watching a TV monitor scroll out information. A studio research guy is making notes, cocking his head to one side, looking mysterious.

ME

What does all this mean?

STUDIO GUY

It means that women love the show. Men like the show.

ME

What does *that* mean?

STUDIO GUY

It means you're on the air. And in a good time slot.

ME

What?

STUDIO GUY
(grinning)

With numbers like these, the network can't say no.

DISSOLVE TO:

INT. OUR OFFICE—DAY

We are overjoyed. We throw caution to the wind. We begin reading spec scripts. We begin meeting writers. We begin hearing rumors.
SFX: Phone rings.

INTERCUT WITH:

INT. REGENCY HOTEL—DAY

My agent is in a suite, on the phone. Other members of the agency are in the background, on different phones. They are in New York for the traditional fall schedule announcements.

                    MY AGENT
          What do you hear?

                    ME
          We're on the air. And in a good time slot.

                    MY AGENT
          Who told you that?

                    ME
          The studio guy. The research guy.

                    MY AGENT
          Because of the *testing*? Don't tell me
          you're listening to that crap?

                    ME
               (small voice)
          But he said . . .

                    MY AGENT
          I hear not so good things. I hear you're a
          long shot.

                    ME
               (small voice)
          But women love us.

                    MY AGENT
               (soothing, comforting)
          I know they do, honey. I know they do.
          But listen, if this doesn't work out, it's no

big deal. You'll get a show on the air.
Eventually. Maybe not this one. Or the
next. But the one after that. Probably.

                    ME
But the testing . . .

                 MY AGENT
Shut up about the goddamn testing! It's
meaningless!

                    ME
But why would the studio spend money
on something that was meaningless? Why
would they waste their money?

                 MY AGENT
You're not seriously asking me that
question, are you? It's a *studio*.

                    ME
Oh.

                 MY AGENT
               (suddenly upbeat)
But listen, if I'm wrong, and they do buy
the show, I have one client who's just
great! He's just great! I'll set up a meeting!

                              DISSOLVE TO:

INSERT SHOT:

A PAGE FROM *VARIETY*—
    listing all of the produced pilots in
    contention for slots on the fall schedule.
    Each is grouped by network, with its
    producer/creators listed, and a short
    log-line.

MY FINGER RUNS DOWN THE LIST—

and stops at our show, and its description:

Five guys live together in NYC apartment.

PULL BACK:

INT. OUR OFFICE—CONTINUOUS

I smile, close Variety. *Look up, concerned. Something is troubling me. I open* Variety *once more.*

CUT TO:

INSERT SHOT:

SAME *VARIETY* PAGE—

I look over the list again.

MY FINGER RUNS DOWN THE LIST—

Stops at another listing under our network's heading. The description reads:

Young people hanging out together in NYC.

PULL BACK:

INT. OUR OFFICE—CONTINUOUS

My complexion turns sickly green. I realize that the network has two similar shows in competition. Ours, "Five guys . . ."; and theirs, "Young people . . ."

ME
(muttering darkly)
We're dead.

CUT TO:

INT. MY PLACE—DAY

Nine a.m. I am sitting in my underwear, drinking a cup of coffee.

MY AGENT (O.S.)
I just heard. It didn't happen.

ME
Oh.

MY AGENT
Sorry, kid.

ME
Yeah. They went with "Young people . . ."
didn't they?

MY AGENT
They may want it for midseason. Or they
may just let their option expire.

ME
When does it expire?

MY AGENT
January first, 1995.

ME
What?

MY AGENT
But maybe sooner. I'll call you right back.

DISSOLVE TO:

INT. MY PLACE—DAY

I stare out over the Pacific.

DISSOLVE TO:

INT. MY PLACE—DAY

Later. I'm still staring.
SFX: Phone rings.

MY AGENT (O.S.)

I've got good news, and bad news, and just
news.

ME

You have bad news? I thought I already
got the bad news.

MY AGENT

There's always worse news. Always.

ME

What is it?

MY AGENT

The network released the show. They've
given up their option.

ME

Actually, right now, that sounds like good
news to me. At least it's over.

MY AGENT

It's not over. That's the just news. Your
studio is starting a network of its own in a
few months. They may want to order the
show for their own network.

ME

So it's not over?

MY AGENT

Nope.

ME

It'll never be over, will it?

MY AGENT

Nope. And that's the good news.

CUT TO:

Which brings us to today. Today we are waiting for the studio to tell us if they want our show. If they do, then I have narrowly escaped eating that karmic shit sandwich. They will order a bunch of shows for their fledgling network, and I will be in the chips again.

In the end, of course, what happened to turn our hot pilot into a nonevent was an inchoate, invisible force that governs Hollywood. Call it the Fade. It didn't die—nothing dies here; nothing, in the words of my agent, is ever over. Things just fade. The obituary page in *Variety* is the perfect embodiment of the Fade. No one who reads it ever exclaims, "Oh, what a shock! So-and-so died!" What one says is, "Oh, what a shock! So-and-so was still alive until last Tuesday. I thought he died *years* ago."

FADE OUT.

Wall Street

FADE IN: JUNE/JULY/AUGUST 1994

The fundamental difference between a Hollywood novice and a sad-eyed veteran is that a novice calls a script a "script," a television show a "television show," and a feature film assignment a "feature film assignment." A veteran calls all of these things, simply, "a piece of business."

I have never been able to pull off that kind of tough business-guy talk without sounding like a complete dork. That, along with my childish insistence on the literal meaning of words such as "contractual obligation," "creative approval," and "prompt payment," have kept my career unswervingly in the slow lane.

CUT TO:

INT. OUR OFFICE—DAY

We are still brooding about our failed pilot. I have scavenged through my garage, rooting through old boxes, to find my film school–era Enemies List. I attach a list of the network's upper-level executives. I show the list to Dan.

DAN
You forgot one name.

He takes the list from me and writes the name of the guy from the studio who told us, after the test results came in, that "we were on the air and in a good time slot."

Dan taps the list with intensity, then circles the studio guy's name with his index finger.

>   DAN (CONT'D)
>   *(with great feeling)*
> Him I want dead.

SFX: Phone rings.

INTERCUT WITH:

EXT. ORSO RESTAURANT—DAY

My agent is on the curb, talking on a cell phone, waiting for the valet to bring the car. Orso has a notorious valet-parking problem.

>   MY AGENT
> How are we looking?

>   ME
> Sorry?

>   MY AGENT
> Are you excited?

>   ME
> About what?

>   MY AGENT
> About what. About what, he says. About your show.

>   ME
> You mean the show that didn't sell?

>   MY AGENT
> It did too sell.

                          ME
     No it didn't.

                      MY AGENT
     Not to the originally intended buyer, no.

My agent waves a valet parking stub at the attendant.
He takes Robert Shapiro's ticket first.

                          ME
     You know what? This conversation is
     giving me a cluster headache.

                      MY AGENT
     Have you tried reverse-reflexology shiatsu
     energy-massage?

                          ME
     No.

                      MY AGENT
     I have a person. He'll come to your house.
     I'll set it up.

                          ME
     What's all this about the show being sold?

                      MY AGENT
     Your show was sold? Great!
     Congratulations!

                          ME
     I'm asking *you.*

                      MY AGENT
     Hey, I haven't heard a thing. It's a quiet
     time. People are out of town or watching
     the O.J. Simpson trial.

My agent nods curtly to Shapiro.

ME

But—

MY AGENT

What I *do* know is that when I started in
this business, I had a little office over a
sewing store on Ventura Boulevard.

ME

And?

MY AGENT

Look at me now. Not bad, huh?

A long pause.

ME

But—

MY AGENT

You didn't let me finish. When I started
out in this business there were only two
big buyers in town, only two big
networks. ABC was the third, and that
was the new kid on the block. And now
look at it. The number one network. I'm
happy for them, I really am. I wonder if I
should retire soon?

Another long pause.

ME

Hello?

MY AGENT

The point is, if you could stop interrupting
me for five seconds please, the point is
that by January 1995 there will be *six*
buyers for television product. Six. That's
almost three times as many. Six big

networks. Now if we can't get your show
on at least one of them, then . . . well,
maybe you should change careers.

*My agent laughs. Smiles and waves at Shapiro as he
drives away.*

                    ME
Or maybe you should.

                MY AGENT
What did I do to deserve that?

                    ME
It was a joke.

                MY AGENT
You should seek therapy. For the
darkness.

                    ME
It was a joke.

                MY AGENT
Your industry is in turmoil and you're
cracking jokes. You've got a failed pilot
that your studio is desperately shilling
around town and yet you see fit to crack
wise. Interesting response.

                    ME
But—

                MY AGENT
Stop interrupting me.

                    ME
But—

The valet roars up with my agent's car.

Gotta go!

CUT TO:

It is rare that a conversation with my agent has a clarifying effect, and yet, as we zigzag from scenario to scenario, the picture that emerges—distorted, jangling, fragmented, chaotic—is an accurate depiction of the television business in 1994. My agent is correct: there are now, or are soon to be, six broadcast television networks. As I write this, at least two of the older ones, CBS and ABC, are rumored to be takeover targets. The antitrust regulations that have prevented the networks from owning the shows—sorry, the *pieces of business*—on their airwaves are almost fully repealed.

EXT. STUDIO PARKING LOT—DAY

Blazing sunlight. 2:00 p.m. I've just pulled into the parking lot. I run into a studio executive walking back to his office from lunch at the commissary. I am trying, through my body language, to imply that I too am returning from lunch, albeit off the lot. The truth is that I am coming into the office for the first time today.
We exchange pleasantries. I wonder if the exec notices my wet hair.

STUDIO EXEC
Are you happy in your office?

ME
Right now?

STUDIO EXEC
No, I mean in general.

ME
I suppose.

STUDIO EXEC
But they're not large enough for
production offices, are they?

ME
We're not in production.

STUDIO EXEC
You will be soon.

ME
(interested)
Yeah? What have you heard?

STUDIO EXEC
I hear they're about to order your show.

ME
For which network?

STUDIO EXEC
I'd rather not say.

ME
Meaning you don't know?

STUDIO EXEC
(testy)
Look, do you want to move into a bigger
suite of offices or don't you?

ME
Yeah, yeah, sure, sure.

STUDIO EXEC
Okay then. We'll move you over the
weekend. Jesus Christ, your agent is
right. You *are* impossible to deal with.

CUT TO:

And so we move—me, Dan, our assistant, and six bottles of gin—to larger, nicer, fully decorated offices. The carpet is soft and fluffy. Our conference room (a conference room!) is tastefully arranged. The lighting is understated. I am struck with the realization that we have moved into production offices for a show that doesn't have a production order from a network that doesn't yet exist.

CUT TO:

INT. MAPLE DRIVE RESTAURANT—DAY

Lunch with an agent from another agency. I am suddenly struck by how far we've come in the business: this kind of thing no longer makes me nervous, furtively tearing my bread into tiny strips, eyes darting around the place, looking for spies.
In fact, we're having lunch with this agent as "industry professionals," since we, at least in theory, are looking to hire writers for a show that, in theory, might get an order from a network that, in theory, might start up in a few months.
Cheers *seems a million years in the past.*

AGENT
Do you have any idea how hot you guys
are right now?

ME
Hot how?

AGENT
Hot hot, that's how.

ME
Hot hot?

AGENT
When I started in this business there were
only four buyers—just four.

ME
You're twenty-eight.

AGENT
Believe me, I know. I feel it every day. The point is, pretty soon there'll be six buyers—and that's just broadcast networks. All the big cable stations will have original programming too. And they all want to be in business with you two. You're hot. Hot hot.

ME
Why?

AGENT
Because you have an unsold pilot. Not everybody can say that.

ME
Yeah. Some people can say that they have a *sold* pilot.

AGENT
You know what I think? I think success is overrated. It ties you down. Which would you rather have: a successful show on a big network, grinding you down every day, every day a new crisis, a star tantrum, an affiliates rebellion, a script rewrite; or, would you rather have a dozen unsold pilots, each for a different network, each a new, fresh adventure?

ME
Ummm . . .

AGENT
You make more money in failure.

                         ME

Really? I would?

                       AGENT

Not with your agent, no. But if you sign
with me, absolutely. You guys are hot. Hot
hot hot.

                         ME

Hot hot *hot*?

                       AGENT

Okay, so I exaggerate.

                                    CUT TO:

And so, as we wait for our production order from a network
that has yet to birth itself, and after a few desultory afternoons
rattling around our new suite of offices, we begin writing a feature film. It's July, when a young man's fancy turns to pieces of
business. And we have lunch with a bunch of other writers.

                                    CUT TO:

INT. CITRUS RESTAURANT—DAY

*About five writers are sitting around a table, each
eating identical chicken salads and gossiping about
people in the business, some of whom are in the restaurant at the time, a few of them within earshot.*

                         ME

Have you heard this thing about the six
networks?

                      WRITER #1

I heard seven.

                      WRITER #2

I heard six, but with a seventh cable thing.

_____

                         115

WRITER #3

(spotting someone across the dining room)
See that asshole? That fucking no-talent
moron wrote some stupid movie about
some goddamn bomb or something.

He waves cheerily across the room at the no-talent
moron.

WRITER #3 (CONT'D)

(smiling through clenched teeth, waving)
Hi, asshole. Hi, no-talent fuck.

WRITER #4

What do you care?

WRITER #3

It opened last Friday. Made twenty-three
million dollars its first weekend.

WRITER #4

Yikes.

WRITER #2

What am I doing in this business?

WRITER #1

Interactive, my friends. Multimedia. The
wave of the future.

ME

What's that?

WRITER #1

I'm into a deal now in the interactive
action genre for home-based multimedia
distribution. And I'm making a mint, let
me tell you.

ME

You mean you're writing video games?

WRITER #1

Basically, yes.

ME

Wow.

WRITER #1

The future is now, buddy. Seven
networks. One hundred channels of
programming. Decentralized feature film
production. Video games, CD-ROMs,
Nintendo, Sega . . . somebody has got to
write that crap. They can get a computer
to direct it. A cartoon to act in it. But you
need a living, breathing, actual hack to
write it.

CUT TO:

The chaotic nature of the entertainment industry has done
what no amount of melodramatic Oscar-night speeches, fifties-
era blacklist reminiscences, or embittered and disorganized
Writers Guild meetings have yet been able to achieve. The
writer in Hollywood, thanks to an explosion of ministudios, new
media, and high-stakes competition, is actually an important
commodity. You're no longer a TV writer or feature writer or
home shopping club writer; you're a "content provider." And
everyone wants to be in business with you, even if you suck.
Maybe especially if you suck. This glorious industry, the business, the town—whatever we call it this week—is a huge, colorful mosaic made up of glittering, golden pieces of business.

CUT TO:

INT. OUR NEW OFFICE—DAY

*The O.J. Simpson preliminary hearings are on televi-
sion. Work has stopped for the day.*
SFX: Phone rings.

INTERCUT WITH:

INT. MY AGENT'S OFFICE

The TV is on there too, and tuned to the hearings. The sound echoes strangely through the telephone wire, creating a weird old-movie-Nazi-siren kind of Doppler effect.

                    MY AGENT
          Are you excited?

                    ME
          Yes, actually. Did you know that with six
          new networks, and cable, and
          decentralized feature film production, the
          business is swimming with opportunities
          for writers?

                    MY AGENT
                    (sarcastic)
          Did I know that? How should I know that?
          I only spend ten hours a day on the phone
          with everyone from Michael Eisner to
          Alan Suess's maid.

                    ME
          Who?

                    MY AGENT
          Exactly!
                    (then, muttering)
          Did I know that. Did I know that.
                    (loudly)
          I'm the one who told you that! I'm the one
          who told you that the future of this
          business is wide open. You can do
          anything.

ME

We're writing a feature.

MY AGENT

Except that. There's no real money in features.

ME

Fine. We'll move on to another piece of business.

MY AGENT

Another *what*?

ME

Another piece of business.

Long pause.

MY AGENT

You took my advice and got yourself some therapy, right?

ME

Nope.

MY AGENT

You saw my reverse-reflexology shiatsu energy-massage guy?

ME

Nope.

MY AGENT

Well, whatever you did, you've got a whole new attitude.

ME

Thanks.

MY AGENT

That wasn't really a compliment. By the

way, the studio called this morning.
They're anticipating an order for your
series, for thirty episodes.

                    ME
Thirty?

                    MY AGENT
Yep.

                    ME
Isn't that a lot?

                    MY AGENT
Yep.

                    ME
Won't that cut into my other . . .

                    MY AGENT
Pieces of business? Yes, it will.

                    ME
But I thought—

                    MY AGENT
Hey, no offense, but you aren't really big
enough yet for pieces of business. Wait a
few years, and maybe after this show fails,
and another show fails, and maybe you
have a few more unsold pilots, *then* maybe
it'll be pieces of business time.

                                        CUT TO:

A friend and I are on the way to the studio one morning when
we stop off at a local restaurant for a cup of coffee and a blue-
berry muffin. The restaurant is called Campanile, and at night
it's a pretty swank place. But in the morning, in an effort to
develop what we in the entertainment industry call "ancillary
markets," the proprietors serve a light breakfast. By "light" I

mean the food, not the price; coffee and a muffin runs around ten dollars. In the parking lot, my friend runs into an old friend of his, someone he has not seen in many years.

                                                    CUT TO:

EXT. CAMPANILE RESTAURANT PARKING
LOT—DAY

The two old friends shake hands and smile.

                        MY FRIEND
            Hello there.

                        HIS FRIEND
            Hi.

                        MY FRIEND
            How are you?

                        HIS FRIEND
                        (shrugging)
            Movie.

                                                    CUT TO:

Movie. He's movie. By which, I slowly understand, he means "I'm working on a movie, thanks for asking." In a way, he has simplified a worn-out Hollywood conversation: hi-how-are-you-what-are-you-working-on? Dogs sniff genitals; we say, "What-are-you-working-on?"

The other possibility, one slightly more embittering, is that the old friend knows that my friend is working in television and has been for years, and that *he* is working in film, or what we call *features*, and that he wants him to know it. Television people and feature people have an ancient cold war of status always raging beneath the surface of any encounter. Feature people have a kindly, aristocratic disdain for television people. When they compliment us, it is usually with a condescending admiration, i.e., "I can't *believe* that you go into the studio every day and work work

work. Really, you people are just a little *factory*. How marvelous! I could *never* do what you do. I need time to *think* about my work, to *noodle*, to *refine*. How lucky for you that you don't!"

Television people comfort themselves with their larger pay-checks. The bitterness, though, grows. Feature people—who seem only to be able to make movies based on television shows—look down on television people for the same reason that old money sniffs at new money and the upper class shrinks from the middle class: we're new, we're loud, and there are more of us. The balance sheet of any major Hollywood studio embroiders the point: huge losses in the feature side are balanced by huge profits in the television side. *Full House* covers *Waterworld*. (Or, almost.) The only reason TV people don't make more trouble is that they all want to work in features.

                                                              CUT TO:

INT. MY PLACE—DAY

Dan and I are fed up with waiting around the office for a series order from the network that our studio is starting—or saying that it's starting. We elect to wait around at home instead.

Instead of relaxing, I am seized with the need to telephone my agent.

I grab the phone, dial, talk to my agent's assistant, wait a few moments. My agent comes on the line.

                          ME
          We're thinking about writing a feature
          film spec.

                      MY AGENT
          Wonderful. That's a terrific idea. Do you
          know why?

                          ME
          Why?

MY AGENT

You'll get it out of your system. You'll
write one, it won't sell, and it'll be out of
your system. And that will be good.
Because you'll *never never ever* get
another chance to write one.

ME

What?

MY AGENT

Please. You'll be busy. You'll be producing
your television show or pitching another
show or working on someone else's
television show.

ME

But—

MY AGENT

We are not having a conversation. I am
talking.

ME

But—

MY AGENT

It's a bad career move. It's a waste of time.

ME

But—

MY AGENT

Plus I don't handle feature scripts. It
would be handled by someone else at the
agency and do you know what? There's
nobody here as nice as me.

CUT TO:

Wall Street and my agent agree on one thing: television is where the action is. The finance pages of the newspaper brim each day with the latest takeover gossip: Disney is going to buy CBS, unless it buys NBC, unless Time Warner buys NBC, which they won't if they can buy ABC, which won't be sold unless the buyer can come up with *$15 billion*, which no one can unless the Viacom-Blockbuster deal goes through, which it may, which means that NBC is on the block, unless the Japanese sell MCA or Columbia/Tri-Star, which they'll have to, because to own a network you have to be an American, which is why Rupert Murdoch turned in his green card for a passport, and to own a network you need *$15 billion*, which is, how you say, *real heavy coin*.

Young people are heading to Los Angeles in the kind of droves that, ten or fifteen years ago, choked and clogged Wall Street. Doltish college kids with no imagination don't want to be just investment bankers anymore; they want to be *entertainment sector analysts* and *new media venture capitalists* and *film industry bankers*. It's as if everyone in the 212 area code woke up one day, and said, "Hey, look at all those people in Los Angeles making all that money. Me too! Gimme!" and so here they are.

Two big studios are starting new networks of their own. One of them has had the good sense to schedule our little series.

The order came in for thirteen episodes. The new media world order was so far turning out to be a disappointment. It was a lot like the *old* media world order: things happened slowly, the number of episodes was never as high as you expected, and ultimately, more networks meant only more network executives.

Nevertheless, we excitedly set to work. We hire a staff of writers. We hire a production crew and a line producer. We get busy writing scripts. Things are busy in our little beehive, and in quiet, reflective, cigar-smoking moments, Dan and I allow ourselves to daydream a bit. "What if," we think to ourselves, "what if this new media world order means that everything gets organized? What if the fact that our studio is a part owner of a new network means that everyone acts like he's on the same team? What if the network executives are nice and easy to deal with? What if they order plenty of episodes—not teeny numbers like nine and twelve, but big, *big* numbers like twenty-two—which would be a full-season order—and forty-four?" Cigar smoke clouds the office as we muse: "And since the studio wants nothing more than to make enough episodes to syndicate the series, and since they own the network, why stop at forty-four?" Getting excited: "Why not make fifty right off the bat? Why not sixty? Why not one hundred? Sure," we think, "being an obscure show on a start-up network isn't a prestige gig, but it will be lucrative, as in lucre, lots of filthy lucre."

                                                        CUT TO:

INT. OUR NEW OFFICE—DAY

SFX: Phone rings.

INTERCUT WITH:

EXT. RITZ CARLTON LAGUNA NIGUEL—DAY

My agent is sitting by the pool.

                          MY AGENT
            Hi! The weather is great!

                            ME
            Where are you?

                          MY AGENT
            On vacation. For the holidays.

                            ME
            Which holidays?

                          MY AGENT
            The *Jewish* holidays.

                            ME
            Which holiday?

MY AGENT
You're an Episcopalian. A WASP. What do
you know from Jewish holidays?

ME
I know some Jewish holidays. Try me.

MY AGENT
What is this, the Inquisition? Am I on
trial? My God, I am on trial. This I cannot
believe.

ME
I'm just asking you which Jewish holiday
it is that you're celebrating.

MY AGENT
The Festival of Schmutblech.

ME
What?

MY AGENT
Okay so I made it up. I'm not allowed a
day off apparently.

ME
I was just curious—

MY AGENT
I called you with good news and you
instantly attack me.

ME
What's the good news?

MY AGENT
I forget. I'm all turned around now.

ME

Was it . . . something about my feature
spec? Because I've been thinking and it
occurred to me that if I take a year off
from tele—

MY AGENT

Oh yeah. I remember. They just hired a
head of the network. And the good news
is that the guy they hired has never heard
of you or your show.

ME

Why is that good news?

MY AGENT

Because the other person they were
considering hates you and your work.

ME

Hates?

MY AGENT

Don't obsess. That person is no longer in
the running. Your job now is to maintain
as low a profile as possible and shoot as
many shows as possible as quickly as
you can.

ME

But—

MY AGENT

I've got to go. It's time for the service.

CUT TO:

The next day, the *Wall Street Journal* reports that my studio is
actively bidding for a network. This is confusing, because up to
that morning, I thought my studio was starting one of its own.

"What if," we daydream darkly, "what if all this talk about the new media world order is a load of crap?"

CUT TO:

EXT. STUDIO PARKING LOT—DAY

We run into a studio executive as we are walking to our office from the studio commissary. (Now that we're in preproduction, we get in early.)

STUDIO EXEC
Hi.

ME
Hi.

A long pause. We walk in silence for a bit.

STUDIO EXEC
I want you to come to a party.

ME
I'd like to come to your party.

STUDIO EXEC
Not *my* party. *A* party.

ME
Okay.

STUDIO EXEC
The new head of the new network is giving a party for all of the new shows.

ME
All? There are only three.

STUDIO EXEC
Two. One was canceled this morning, so they're not invited.

ME

Canceled? But we haven't even
premiered yet.

STUDIO EXEC

I didn't say it was going to be a fun party.

CUT TO:

The next week, the *Wall Street Journal* publishes a special
section on the new television industry. It handicaps the various
takeover battles. Our new network is mentioned, prefixed by
the adjective "fledgling." Our new network chief is mentioned,
prefixed by the adjective "demanding." Our show is mentioned
without a prefix. I am unaccountably—and foolishly—cheered.
Publicity, in that weird logic that only Hollywood and Wall
Street appreciate, somehow protects us. They can't cancel a
show, we reason, that's been mentioned in the *Wall Street
Journal.*

CUT TO:

EXT. OUR NEW OFFICE—DAY

I am heading out the door.
SFX: Cell phone chirps.
I look around guiltily and take out my cell phone. A few
years ago, I didn't even own one. Until a few months
ago, I never would have taken it out of my car. And
until very, very recently, I wouldn't have left it on. But
I've come a long way since Cheers, *longer since film*
school, vast distances since being an English major at
Yale. So now not only do I own a cell phone, but I leave
it on, people call me on it, I have conversations on
it. . . .

I answer the phone. Yale and my Yankee roots fade far-
ther into the foggy past.

ME
Did you see our mention in the *Wall Street Journal*?

MY AGENT
See it? Who do you think planted it?

ME
You planted it?

MY AGENT
No, I'm asking you: who do you think planted it? It's not good.

ME
Not good? It's great!

MY AGENT
No, it's not.

ME
But everybody reads the *Journal*.

MY AGENT
No. Everybody reads *Variety*. New York money people read the *Journal*. So they read about your show and then they hype it. You're the guys from *Cheers*. You're hit machines. You're cutting edge, new, now. The word goes out that your show is a surefire hit and everybody expects great things. Snag: you're on a brand-new network, and the best—the very best— you can hope for is a three or four ratings point. But the New York money people don't know that because they don't know from this business—people who read *Variety* know from this business, people who read the *Wall Street Journal do not*

know from this business! So when your
show gets a four and you're popping
champagne, the New York money people
are wringing their hands and spreading
doom and gloom and the studio stock
goes down and they get nervous and
cancel your show.

ME
Why am I not in the feature film business?

MY AGENT
What? You're not having fun?

CUT TO:

I hustle to my car and race home. I am the recent owner of an
eleven-week-old puppy, who, when not chewing on an electric
cord with 110 volts crackling through it, expresses his contempt
for me by shitting in out-of-the-way places in my house. I catch
him squatting over the special television section of the *Wall
Street Journal* and staring at me in a casual way. My dog, I
realize by the way he treats anything to do with television, is a
feature person. Ours will be a turbulent relationship.

FADE OUT.

Executive Inaction

___

FADE IN: OCTOBER/NOVEMBER 1994

We are in production, fulfilling a thirteen-episode order. One year has passed since our initial pitch, and the months in between have led a rocky trail to this month, to production, to what, in our innocence, we thought would be fun. It *is* fun, of course, but it is also hard work. My father has two sayings he likes to repeat:

1. *"Every* job is a sales job."

and

2. *"Everything* you really want to do turns out to be hard work."

CUT TO:

INT. OUR OFFICE—DAY

Our offices have been transformed. Where once we romped in solitary splendor (three people, six rooms), we now need to find space for our assistant, two writing assistants, a production assistant ("PA" in industry parlance), two staff writers, a few consultants, and another producer.

It's not a packed house, but it's close.

___

SFX: *Phone rings.*
The PA answers it, heads down the hall to the writers'
room, shouting.

> PA
>
> Run-through!

TRACKING SHOT:

The PA brushes by the staff writers, who are holding
mugs of coffee and the "trades"—Variety, *the* Hollywood Reporter. *As he passes them:*

> PA (CONT'D)
>
> Run-through!

The writers sigh, toss the trades, grab script binders and
pencils, and head for the door.
The PA turns a corner and enters.

INT. THE WRITERS' ROOM—CONTINUOUS

where I am sitting with Dan and a consultant.

> PA (CONT'D)
> *(shouting)*
>
> Run-through!

> ME
>
> Yes, thanks. We heard. Give us five
> minutes.

> PA
>
> But they just called "run-through."

> ME
>
> Yes, and in five minutes, we'll walk over to
> the stage.

> PA
>
> But the director called it for now.

ME
(slowly, staying calm)
Yeah, I know, but it's going to take us five
minutes to wrap up what we're doing
here, and walk over to the stage.

PA
Won't that upset the director?

ME
Excuse me?

PA
Won't that upset him? Won't that
undermine his authority?

ME
What? Where did you learn that kind of
shit? Huh, kid?

The "kid" is four years younger than I.

PA
Well, isn't the director in charge of the
production?

ME
This production? The one *my partner and
I* are in charge of?

PA
Um . . .

ME
That director? The one my partner and I
hired?

It's been a long, long, long time since Cheers.

PA
Um . . .

                    ME
Where'd you learn that crap, kid?

"Kid" again. I'm becoming an Industry Asshole.

                    PA
Um . . . UCLA Film School, I guess.

                    ME
            (suddenly chastened)
Oh, yeah. Right.

SFX: Phone rings.
The PA lunges for it, happy to be out of our conversa-
tion. He answers it, waits a beat, turns to me with a sly
smile.

                    PA
Your agent on line two.

I grab the phone.

                MY AGENT
Hi.

                    ME
Hi.

                MY AGENT
You sound busy.

                    ME
I am busy. We're shooting episode four
tonight, and they just called "run-
through."

                MY AGENT
Well, you sound busy. My advice is, take
some time for you. Pamper yourself.

                    Me
Is that why you called?

MY AGENT

To tell you to pamper yourself? Give me a break.

Long pause.

ME

Then why did you call?

MY AGENT

I'm coming to the show tonight!

ME

And?

MY AGENT

And I need to make sure that the PA stocks lots and lots of those small Evian bottles backstage.

ME

Why?

MY AGENT

In case I'm thirsty, that's why.

ME

Yes, I guess I can see your point.

MY AGENT

Plus I'd like to take some home. They're so convenient. Anyway, you'd better get to run-through. You don't want to piss off the director.

CUT TO:

Let me tell you a true story about Hollywood.

Two men have been friends and writing partners for many, many years. They have endured more than their share of career tumult. For many years they were successful writers and pro-

136

ducers, and had earned the lucrative status of show runner twice over. Show runner is the delightful and colorful phrase used by executives and networks to denote those few writers who can, in their estimation, run shows—that is, hire and fire writing staff, supervise casting and production, and guide scripts from conception to rewriting to postproduction.

What show runners don't have to do is write. Naturally, all television writers aspire to be show runners.

Back to the story.

After a few more ups than downs, the partners find themselves on the short end of a bad deal at a notoriously nasty studio, running six episodes of an egregious sitcom starring a clinically insane harridan has-been. This kind of thing happens all the time.

So somewhere mid–sixth episode, after ten weeks of studio and network interference, and after a particularly stressful conference call between the network executive and the studio executive, both of whom agreed on only one thing—namely, that neither partner was, in their estimation, much of a show runner—one partner locks the other partner in his office and proceeds to beat him senseless with a desk lamp. The victimized partner (but aren't they both, in a sense, victims?) lands in the hospital, the lamp-wielding partner is fired (there is, amazingly enough, a no-starting-of-fights clause in that particular studio's standard contract), production is shut down for a week or two, and every other writer in town has something to talk about at lunch.

That story, like most of the stories I tell in these pages, is *mostly* true. Who knows, really, what happened in that locked office? And who knows, really, what the dynamic relationship was between those two partners? Maybe the guy who got cranked with the lamp *deserved* to be cranked with the lamp. I don't know. When hauled before a judge, as a defendant in two lawsuits (one from the studio, for something called "infringement and/or arrestation of production schedule due to malice and/or negligence"; and one from his former partner), the desk lamp warrior gave this as his reason for the attack: "He didn't back me up in a meeting with the network." At lunchtime gatherings of writers, two camps quickly form: those who think, "Okay, he didn't back you up in a meeting, fine, that's not so good, but perhaps you could have stopped just short of embedding glass splinters in his eye"; and those who think, "Okay, he didn't back you up in a meeting, why did you let him live?"

Dan and I are currently about four episodes into a twelve-episode order. Were he to beat me knee-walking bloody with a table lamp, I assure you, I will have deserved it. Producing a television show plunges even the slickest show runner into a personal *Apocalypse Now*, with everything from budget overruns to explosive dysentery.

Production does something else too: it delineates the outside edge of acceptable social behavior. I have seen producers dribble sauce from a takeout lunch on their chins and clothes, and then bark rudely at the nearest PA to fetch some napkins; I have seen producers too lazy to mutter even the most cursory "thank you"; and I have seen producers literally *walk away* while someone of a lower caste on the production budget tries to make polite chitchat. Thus, when Dan and I remember merely to mumble our thank-yous and maintain our zombie smiles, we develop the reputation of being "really nice guys." We don't intend to be "really nice guys"; we'd rather be "really fiercely intimidating guys." In a business famous for its screamers and tantrum-tossers, we feel guilty when we snap irritably at a PA.

The true fault line, however, is the one that runs between me and Dan. We've been friends since college—a full ten years—and we woke up one day to discover that we weren't really friends in the conventional sense. What we are is business partners who happen to be friends. Early in our career, we spent a great deal of time together after work and on weekends; later, as the work got harder and the headaches more frequent, I would see him occasionally, usually at the instigation of his wife, of whom I'm extremely fond; at a certain point during the final season of *Cheers*, we barely functioned as partners at all, sharing the producing duties with two other writers. Now, with a year of development under our belt and a large production order to fill, the scale has tipped a bit, and with only each other to rely upon, we've strengthened the weave of our partnership. No one really knows the intricate dynamics of a writing partnership, especially the partners. They muddle their way through, happy to split a paycheck for the privilege of being allowed to play "good cop" ("Sure! Sounds great! Let me check it out with my partner, though") and "bad cop" ("No *fucking* way!") on alternate days.

The complexities of this particular partnership elude me, as I'm sure they elude Dan. Simply put, we check and balance each other. We are the pin to the other's balloon. Our partnership works because we can trust ourselves to be wrong at least 50 percent of the time, and when we're lucky, one guy's time to be wrong coincides with the other's time to be right. Usually, we're both wrong at the same time.

Laughter is a universal indicator: as long as I can still make Dan laugh, things are okay. So far, we're still laughing. The purely creative part of the job—the sitting-on-a-couch-making-jokes part—has always come easy to us. But there's another part to running a show, a larger part, in which I've often failed him. Making critical judgments, organizing a staff, being judicious and careful—these are all areas in which I fall short, occasionally to his irritation, but more often to his undying patience. That he can do all that and still be a dazzlingly talented and funny writer can only be chalked up to luck. Mine, not his.

Truthfully, for us, production is a tropical cruise compared to development. And along the way, against all expectations, our relationship with the cast has developed into an easy, casual, very pleasant system—and in a few instances, outright friendship.

How different from *Cheers*! We're working with actors who are, to a person, poorer than we are. (Crass, yes, but this is Hollywood—these things matter.) And when we walk onto the set, we're regarded with a full measure of either fear or respect—I've never been able to tell the difference, if there is a difference.

CUT TO:

INT. OUR OFFICE—DAY

We're watching the second cut of an episode. We need to lift two minutes to deliver the show at the proper length. The show usually films about five minutes long, which allows us to cut out jokes that don't work, pick up the pace, and fix technical problems.

I see the red light on my phone flash. Then, as the PA answers it, it stays a solid red for a few moments, then flashes again: whoever called is now on hold.

The PA enters.

PA

Agent on line one.
I take a deep breath and answer it.

MY AGENT

I just saw the rough cut of your first episode.

ME

Really?

MY AGENT

Do you have a pencil?

ME

Why?

MY AGENT

I have some notes.

ME

What?

MY AGENT
In scene B, after the woman exits, double
cut to a reaction three-shot—

ME
I'm sorry. I'm not clear on this. *You* have
notes?

MY AGENT
Yes. I have notes. Now, in scene B, after
the reaction, play the rest of the run in a
flat two-shot lifting all the intercuts—

ME
I guess I'm having a hard time processing
this. Since when do agents give notes on a
rough cut?

MY AGENT
They don't. It's not in their purview.

ME
So . . . ?

MY AGENT
So it's in *mine* and I *do*. Get a pencil.

CUT TO:

The entertainment industry is run on pretty much the same
lines as the rest of corporate America, except in the entertainment industry, job performance counts for a good deal less. It's
crucial, early on, to sniff out the cobweb of relationships among
studio executives and between them and the network. Sometimes the top executive has a better relationship with someone
way, way down the ladder than he does with his second-in-
command. So when the guy at the bottom has a note, you have
to listen—or at least, fake listening more energetically. And
when the second-in-command has a note, you fix him with a
steady gaze, let your mind wander, organize your day, whatever.

Because the network holds all the cards, you have to do more than pretend to listen. You have to actually listen. Actually listening to network notes leads, over time, to attacking your partner with a desk lamp.

Now that I think about it, a movie studio doesn't really resemble another corporation so much as it does a large bureaucracy: everyone has a big-shot title; everyone has a big-shot salary; no one does anything. The explosion of titles has become ludicrous—especially after the rash of mergers and buyouts. The closest thing to a big studio in 1994 is a really nasty African military dictatorship: nine thousand generals leading six infantry in a pointless war against twenty nomad tribesmen. Only in this case, the nomad tribesmen are writers, and instead of shooting them or starving them or letting them die of infectious diseases, they pepper them with notes on the script and questions about the rough cut.

Everyone gets to be a president of something—a division ("President of the Network Television Division"); a group ("President of the Domestic Syndication Group of the Network Television Division"); a concept ("President of New Media Concepts for the Domestic Syndication Group of the Network Television Division"); or a vague goal ("President of Entertainment"). Presidents report directly to chairmen, who themselves report to the CEO of the holding company, who reports to the chairmen of the holding company, who report to the *Wall Street Journal*. Everyone else is an executive vice president, except for the kids who deliver the mail, who are just vice presidents. It's grade inflation gone mad: everyone gets firsts in every subject, except those people who have Nobel Prizes.

Luckily for us, we're on a startup network without a meddlesome layer of terrified note-givers in place. And our studio executive is a nice guy about our age, who calls once in a while with a note, and signs off with a hearty "Cool!" when he's through. The best executives are those who have just reached the buck-slip moment of their careers. A buck slip is a piece of heavy-stock stationery about two and a half inches across and six inches long, with the company logo on top, and best of all, your name printed on the bottom. It is literally true that anyone who's anyone in Hollywood has a stack of buck slips. It's the first sign of success. It's the bottom rung of the status-symbol ladder that ends with a shower in your office and a personal chef. Freshly minted executives send out loads and loads of gratuitous mail, just to clip a buck slip to the stack, as if to shout to the world, "Hey world! Look at me! I'm no longer a personal assistant!" Young sharks, slaving away in agency mailrooms or as PAs, have been known to have their own buck slips printed up. It's a lot cheaper than leasing a BMW.

CUT TO:

INT. SOUNDSTAGE—NIGHT

It is Tuesday night and we're shooting our show. The audience is in their seats in the grandstand, but the floor of the stage is crowded with cameras, producers, the director, and about a dozen agents, only some of whom have even the slightest right to be there. Mine, of course, has commandeered the only chair, and is nursing a small bottle of Vittel water—not, as requested, Evian, which was my little way of saying, "Hey, you can't push me around."

The network president and the studio president (or, I should say one of the network presidents and one of the studio presidents) are in a corner trying to watch the show on a small TV monitor. My agent is between them, chattering away merrily, blocking the screen with hand gestures, tugging on their arms to make a point, flailing wildly with the Vittel bottle.

The presidents are trying hard not to hear, straining to see the monitor, working very hard to collect their thoughts and maybe give a few notes for the second take of the scene. But my agent is like a jackhammer at five in the morning: incessant, jangling, nerve shattering, concentration busting. The Vittel bottle takes on a new significance: it wards off dry throat.

TRACKING SHOT:

I walk along the stage apron, passing the cluster of execs and my agent.

> MY AGENT
> So the Republicans control the House and the Senate now. Should be interesting, no?

> STUDIO EXEC
> *(to Network Exec)*
> Maybe this scene would be better if—

> MY AGENT
> My kid did the funniest thing yesterday—

I walk to the edge of the soundstage. In the corner of my eye, I can see my agent still yabbering away, fracturing every attempt the execs make at coherent conversation. I walk back. And hear:

> MY AGENT (CONT'D)
> Want to hear something crazy insane? I liked the Frankenstein movie and *hated* the vampire movie. Nuts, huh?

> NETWORK EXEC
> *(clutching head)*
> Maybe this scene needs—

> MY AGENT
> You want to know my favorite flower? The *iris*. That's it. That's my favorite flower.

> NETWORK EXEC
> Is there any aspirin?

Things get clearer to me. My agent suddenly becomes very wise in my eyes. The evening ends early, and with no notes. I instruct the PA to order several cases of small bottles of Evian.

FADE OUT.

Meet the Press

FADE IN: JANUARY 1995

I heard the following story a few weeks ago:

A while back—let's say, for argument's sake, the mid-seventies—the most popular sitcom on broadcast television featured as its star a famous and versatile comedian, who played a character not unlike himself. One particular episode centered around the character's identical twin brother—played by the comedian himself, utilizing really cheapo split-screen tape effects.

The day of the shoot, a few minutes after a guest audience has thoroughly enjoyed the dress rehearsal, the comedian comes stomping into the writers room, eyes blazing, hands shaking, boiling over with the two most prevalent emotions in Hollywood: incandescent rage and piss-yourself panic. "We're shutting down!" he screams at the writers. "We're going to eat this episode!"

"Why?" they ask.

"Because my brother is getting all the laughs."

Which, when you really really think about it, makes sense.

We are seven days away from the premiere of our new television comedy. The phone rings in what sounds like one continuous chirp from the moment we walk into the office until the second we race to our cars, and worse, the fax machine burps every few minutes with fresh reviews, some from out-of-the-way places like Milwaukee and Baton Rouge, and some from scary places like New York City and Chicago.

When we hear that National Public Radio has called our show a "smart little sitcom," we are elated—too elated, it turns out, for moments later the fax machine spits out a "sitcom without snap" from *People* magazine and a "semifunny" from the *Washington Post*. After lunch, we get an "attractive cynicism" from the *Wall Street Journal* and a "promising new sitcom" from *TV Guide*. Cocktail hour finds us reeling from a "will end up on the manure pile" from the *Boston Globe* and a "skip it" from the *San Diego Union*. The evening comes to a close with a "snappy little sitcom" from the *Hollywood Reporter*, which I enlarge on the office Xerox machine and place next to our "sitcom without snap" from *People*, forming a collage testament to my personal bitterness.

It's strange how much the bad reviews hurt. It's also strange how widely disparate the reviews are—our little show about five guys who share an apartment seems to rub people either the wrong way or the right way, but whatever it does, it rubs them hard. The *New York Daily News* gives us a rave, as do *New York Newsday* and the *New York Post*. *Entertainment Weekly* calls us "uncommonly well-written and acted"; *Variety* rips out our still-beating heart and eats it. The *New York Times* and the *Los Angeles Times* dismiss us so contemptuously that I half expect to be arrested.

Our problem, we rationalize, is that our show *seems* tacky— the *Animal House*–like subject matter—and is on a tacky network, so most reviewers have an awfully hard time getting past the particulars to review the show itself. Also: what fun is it to write a good review, or even a balanced review? I've written reviews before. I know. It's much more fun to draw blood.

CUT TO:

INT. MY CAR—NIGHT

I am heading west on San Vicente Boulevard.

SFX: Cell phone chirps.
I answer it.

INTERCUT WITH:

INT. MY AGENT'S CAR—NIGHT

My agent is heading down Beverly Boulevard.

> MY AGENT
> Congratulations.

> ME
> On what?

> MY AGENT
> Just on being you. On having done it.

> ME
> Done what?

> MY AGENT
> The whole thing. It's marvelous.

> ME
> What are you talking about?

My agent searches the passenger-side seat for a slip of paper.

> MY AGENT
> Look, all it says here on my call sheet is
> Call R.—in re: congratulations. So c'mon,
> meet me fucking halfway here.

> ME
> Look, all I've done today that merits
> congratulations is not put out a contract
> on the guy who writes television reviews
> for *People* magazine, okay?

MY AGENT
Well, see? That's something.

ME
Yeah, well, wait until we hear from the rest of the reviewers.

MY AGENT
Wait wait wait. What do you care what the reviewers say?

ME
What do I care? What do I care what the reviewers say?

MY AGENT
What is this? A David Mamet play? Yes! *What do you care what the reviewers say?*

ME
Well, I—

MY AGENT
Did you *really* think Dustin Hoffman was that great playing the retarded guy in *Rain Man*?

ME
Well . . .

MY AGENT
And wasn't *Schindler's List* kinda *boring*?

ME
Well . . .

MY AGENT
And let's face it: *Murphy Brown* is a bad show. She's got no range and all the other characters do is shout and mug.

ME

But—

MY AGENT

Two words: grow the fuck up.

ME

But I—

MY AGENT

I am not having this conversation. We are
not having this conversation. This
conversation is not being conversed.

ME

You know what? This day is hard enough
without this phone call.

MY AGENT

Don't get huffy. I was calling to
congratulate you and I'm attacked.
Interesting.

ME

You called to congratulate me?

MY AGENT

I did.

ME

About what?

MY AGENT

Do you know who this is?

*My agent mentions the name of a famous trio who have
just started their own studio.*

ME

Yeah, I've heard of them.

MY AGENT
It just so happens that they love you, love
your partner, love your work, and want to
make a deal with you. I told them that you
were busy, that it was out of the question,
that you'd never leave the studio you're at
for any amount of money. Congratulations!

DISSOLVE TO:

INT. MY CAR—NIGHT

*Late at night, when I can't sleep, I drive from my house
at the beach into Hollywood to browse through the only
late-night bookstore in town, Book Soup.*

DISSOLVE TO:

INT. BOOK SOUP—NIGHT

*I feign interest in the New Fiction table, make a few
desultory stabs at the New Nonfiction shelf, but I'm
drawn, like a porn freak to the dark curtained corner of
the newsstand, to the section labeled Movies/Televi-
sion/Industry and to a book entitled* The Encyclopedia
of Short-Lived Television Series. *I always do the same
thing: I check the index to make sure that my name still
isn't there.*

CUT TO:

INT. MY BEDROOM—NIGHT

The room is dark.

SLOW TRACKING SHOT—

through the darkened room.
*SFX: We hear the sound of a pen scratching against
paper.*

THE BATHROOM DOOR, AJAR—

a shaft of light blazes into the bedroom.

TRACKING SHOT INTO THE BATHROOM—

the scratching noise gets louder and louder. Some splashing.

PAN UP TO REVEAL—

me, in the bathtub, sipping bourbon from the bottle, a stack of newsclips forming a soggy pile on one side, a wrinkled old sheet of paper on the other.

INSERT SHOT: THE WRINKLED SHEET OF PAPER—

it is the old Enemies List, with the original names scratched out, and new names, assorted television critics' names, in splotchy columns. Some names are underlined several times.

CUT TO:

Most of the following day is spent furiously courting the press. We're in a tight spot: our show is premiering on a brand-new network. Scrutiny is close. The critics are expecting to see a parade of crap. It's hard to convince them otherwise. We spend the day at something called the Television Critics Association Day at a fancy Los Angeles hotel. The event is high-grade junket—the China White of press tours. The critics get supped and schmoozed and stroked and gifted: a leather binder here, a bottle of wine there, a pen-and-pencil set, a useless baseball cap—and in return they write snide things about our show, tipsy, no doubt, from our wine, bloated from our deli spread. At a certain point in the day, the cast, Dan, and I assemble as a ragtag panel on the dais and field questions from whichever critics aren't in the lobby trying on their new leather jackets, gifts from a large cable channel. The questions are mostly nice, mostly positive. I scan the name tags for a name that matches the New Updated Enemies List. I don't see one, so the afternoon passes without incident.

The next night, we shoot the third-to-last episode of our new series. We hope, of course, that it isn't really the third-to-last; it's the tenth episode of a thirteen-episode preliminary order. We hope, maybe foolishly, that the American public is more in sync with National Public Radio than it is with *People* magazine. We hope that the reviewers from Milwaukee and Boston and San Diego are wrong, and that it is a case of what my writing partner calls the revenge of the people who want to write for television, but never had the courage. We know, of course, that sheer statistics will keep us unknown to most of America. The baby network on which we appear barely covers 75 percent of the country, and our show will be run at odd times on odd channels ("Channel 67, the Voice of Chicklet Valley!").

So we start out with a sense of certain doom, dotted here and there by the faintest sparks of hope. We will certainly be at the bottom of the heap, but perhaps we won't be at the *very* bottom. What we hope for is an industry litotes—that the media won't not like us, that the American people won't unnotice us, that, ultimately, the fledging network on which we appear won't not have nothing to replace us.

CUT TO:

INT. SOUNDSTAGE—NIGHT

We're shooting episode eleven of the twelve-episode order.

This particular episode features roughly six dogs who must, on command, run, jump, sit, and howl. We had been told throughout the week, as the dogs ran wildly through the soundstage licking and nipping and mounting every Teamster electrician on the premises, that they were just nervous, or disoriented, and that come shoot night all would go well. As the cameras roll and the dogs begin licking, nipping, and mounting, I feel a tug at my sleeve.

> MY AGENT
> Hi hi.

> ME
> Hi.

> MY AGENT
> Aren't those dogs the cutest?

> ME
> They'd be cuter if they could hit their marks and do the scene.

> MY AGENT
> If they could hit their marks and do the scene they wouldn't be dogs. They'd be actors.

I laugh at this. My agent laughs too.

> MY AGENT (CONT'D)
> See? I can be funny.

More mayhem onstage. The dog wrangler has cornered most of the dogs in the prop shed. Our regular dog— that is, the lead dog—is sitting on the set quietly fuming. The guest dogs aren't behaving professionally.

> MY AGENT (CONT'D)
> Hear that?

> ME
> Hear what?

> MY AGENT
> Listen.

My agent's head cocks to one side, indicating the studio audience. I notice, for the first time, that they're all

laughing uproariously at the skittering dogs. Big, roll-
ing, chunky laughs—long, air-rich guffaws.

           MY AGENT (CONT'D)
Do you hear? You're a hit!

               ME
But they're not laughing at our show.
They're laughing at some dogs that are
screwing up our show.

            MY AGENT
Same diff.

              ME
What?

            MY AGENT
Look, they're *laughing*, okay? When you
get laughs you take them, no questions
asked. I hope you're getting this on the
track. You never know when you'll need to
goose what you get during the real show.

              ME
But they're not laughing at what we want
them to laugh at.

            MY AGENT
They never are.

                       CUT TO:

   A few nights later, we gather the cast and writing staff
together for our premiere party. It is a low-key event; the cast
bring their families and friends; we all sit around drinking and
eating until it's time to watch our television show broadcast for
the very first time.

INT. PREMIERE PARTY—NIGHT

People stand around in casual groups.
SFX: Party noise: ice in glass, laughter, music.
Dan pulls me aside.

> DAN
>
> Take a look at this.

He hands me a small datebook, "1990" emblazoned on its cover.

> DAN (CONT'D)
>
> I've kept this thing for five years. Look up what happened five years ago today.

I flip through the pages.

CUT TO:

INSERT SHOT:

PAGES—
> flipping by.

MY HAND—
> stops at "January."

FLIPS TO—
> "January 23, 1990."

CUT BACK TO:

INT. PARTY

I look up at Dan.

> ME
> *(softly)*
>
> Man . . .

CUT BACK TO:

INSERT SHOT:

DATE BOOK—
> below the entry for "January 23, 1990" is
> written:

Pitch Meeting @ Cheers
2:00 p.m. Go in through
Melrose Gate

CUT TO:

It was five years ago, to the day, that Dan and I had our first meeting at our first job in television, and took our first step on the long path to this night, to *our* night, to watching our show on broadcast television. I am struck, as I watch the end credits and listen to the toasts of the partygoers, that this is all really happening. That millions of people—not many millions, maybe three—are watching the end credits at the same time. Somehow, all those years on *Cheers* never seemed as real as tonight seems. Tonight, I can feel it in my bones—tonight I have a *career*. Of course, in retrospect, the past five years have been leading inexorably to this night; still, to me it comes as a surprise. Perhaps it's a symptom of being in one's late twenties: tonight I feel like I've turned a corner, but in fact, I turned that corner long ago—I just didn't notice it at the time. I turned it five years ago, when I tossed out my stack of law school applications; I turned it again when I became a producer of *Cheers*. Lucky for me, I didn't notice. My WASP emotional repression has stood me in good stead—had I thought about it, really *thought* about it, I never would have allowed myself to risk the failure, to risk playing in the big ring. And tonight I'm very glad that I did.

FADE OUT.

Dissolve To:

FADE IN: MAY/JUNE 1995

While it is a gross generalization to suggest that comedy writers are mathematically ignorant, it's a fairly safe bet that most of them aren't trained statisticians. Nevertheless, when the ratings come burping out of the office fax, a writer who cannot tell time and who routinely tips 100 percent in restaurants ("Easier to figure out . . . just *double* it") instantly becomes a Compudyne 17mhz 586k Pentium math coprocessor unit.

CUT TO:

INT. OUR OFFICE—DAY

Our second week's ratings come in. Early in the day, we get something called the "Overnights"—ratings based on a dozen or so key major markets (i.e., cities), designed to give a quick snapshot. Later that afternoon, after the Nielsen Company has tabulated its other information (from phone polling, diary sheets, and set-top boxes), it releases the "Nationals"—which become the basis for the weekly rankings.

Each rating is divided into two numbers: the "rating point"—the number of television sets tuned to that program; and the "share point"—the percentage of televisions in use that were tuned to that program. Cheers

regularly garnered a 25 ratings point (each point rep-
resenting, roughly, nine hundred thousand viewers)
and a 32 share.

We are loafing around the writers' room.

The PA enters, holding a few sheets of fax paper.

> PA

Ratings are in.

I take the papers from him, glance at them, then
look up.

> ME

Great numbers!

We have received a 3 rating and a 5 share.

> PA

What did we get?

> ME
> *(insanely cheery)*

A three-five.

> PA

A thirty-five? Great!

> ME

No. A three rating, five share.

> PA

Oh.

> ME

Hey, hey, hey. This is good news. We're
on a start-up network that only reaches
eighty percent of the country. We're on at
nine-thirty, we have a crappy lead-in, I
mean, this is better than they *expected*.
They promised the advertisers a four

share, so we're all way, way ahead.
Plus . . .

I begin shuffling through the pages in sweaty earnest.

                    ME (CONT'D)
          . . . plus, look at our numbers in the key
          major markets—the urban markets,
          where our signal is strongest. We're
          getting a six or seven in the Midwest,
          parts of the South give us a solid four
          rating, New York City loves us. . . .

I reach for a calculator, begin pounding away.

                    ME (CONT'D)
                 (high-pitched; frantic)
          . . . and we're retaining, in most of the
          major markets anyway—but after all,
          that's what we're *talking about here*—
          we're retaining about ninety-five percent
          of our lead-in, which is *pretty fucking good!*
          I mean, we should be celebrating—

Dan slowly removes the sheets from my hands.

                    DAN
                 (quietly)
          The ratings suck, Rob.

                    ME
                 (shouting)
          I know! Don't you think I know that?!

                                      CUT TO:

   Our ratings hold in the three-five range for the duration of
our run. We complete production on our initial order by the
middle of February. What we do now is wait: wait for the network to make up its mind about ordering new episodes; wait for

the studio to swing into action twisting the network's arm; wait, finally, for America to wake herself up and say: "Hey! That's a damn funny show!"

The point of doing a show for a network that is co-owned by the studio is that business partners aren't supposed to screw each other. The point, all those months ago, was that maybe this kind of enterprise signaled a new way of doing business.

What happened was this: in an effort to reduce its near-term losses and reduce its debt after an expensive buyout, our studio sold its interest in the network, essentially cutting us loose. So now we're getting jerked around like everyone else in the business, only in this case, by a fledgling network with only two nights of programming instead of one of the big boys. I don't mind getting screwed over, hell, I *expect* to get screwed over; but I'd like it to be done by a better class of network. Waiting around to hear yes-or-no from a disorganized mess of an enterprise run by an irrational lunatic for bread-crumb-sized stakes takes the joy out of this most joyful business.

We will be waiting for several months. It is axiomatic in Hollywood that any decision that must be made can only be made at the last legal minute. We will hear from the network scant minutes from the moment (June 1, 5:00 p.m.) that our options on the actors' services expire. Unless, of course, America *does* come to her senses and watch our show in busloads, in which case the studio will drag *its* feet in an effort to extort more money from the network. Notice the absence of me in either scenario? It's because at this point, I don't count.

CUT TO:

INT. SANTA MONICA STARBUCKS COFFEE SHOP—DAY

I enter, wearing a pullover emblazoned with the logo of our television show—a "wrap party" gift to the cast and crew.

The wrap party gift is a crucial part of the business,

and one fraught with class implications. Feature films always provide a jacket of some opulence, either leather or heavy cotton, always lined, always expensive. Television shows, depending on their relative success and longevity, satisfy the requirements with a baseball cap, a pullover, or a cheap nylon attaché. Certain shows (your Seinfelds, *your* Cheers*) can't get away with cheaping out, and then you see sprouting all over town* Seinfeld *car coats and* Cheers *jean jackets.*

We're in the very early stages of success (so early, in fact, as to be unrecognizable from failure) and so we passed out pullovers.

I walk up to the counter and order.

ME

Tall latte, please.

GUY BEHIND COUNTER

Sure thing.

He sets about making my coffee, then spots my pullover.

GUY (CONT'D)
(merrily)

Hey! You work on that show?

ME

Yes.

GUY

I love that show! What do you do?

ME

I'm a writer.

GUY

Wow! That's a funny show! That's the funniest show I've ever seen!

                              ME
    Gosh, thanks.

                              GUY
    No, no. Thank *you*.

He hands me my tall latte.

                        GUY (CONT'D)
    So, are you guys, like, looking for any new
    writers? Because, you know, I'm real good
    with dialogue and story is—

                                        DISSOLVE TO:

    A writer friend of mine offers this moral puzzler: You are trav-
eling in the Brazilian rain forest. You come across an aging,
though still spry, Adolf Hitler. You tell him that he is the
greatest villain of the twentieth century and that it will give you
great pleasure to turn him in to the authorities. He tells you that
he's seen your show and he thinks it is "wunderbar." Do you
turn him in?
    Faced with five months of unoccupied waiting time, I become
horrendously ill. This takes all the fun out of staying home
all day.

                                        CUT TO:

INT. MY BEDROOM—DAY

I am watching the Charles Perez Show. *Charles has
on "Men Who Left Their Girlfriends for Their Girlfriends' Brothers."*
SFX: Phone rings.
I groggily answer it.

                        MY AGENT (O.S.)
    How are you feeling?

                              ME
    Well, I'm running a fever and—

MY AGENT

That's terrible—

ME

And I'm dizzy and—

MY AGENT

—but it sounds a lot better than what I had last week. I was dizzy. I ran a fever. Have you seen a doctor? You should get some Percocet.

ME

What's Percocet?

MY AGENT

It's a powerful painkiller. It freezes out the pain receptors in the central nervous system and floods the cerebral cortex with neurological impulses that create a completely restful, drowsy state.

ME

I don't think I need that.

MY AGENT

I wasn't saying get it for *you*.

ME

Why are you calling?

MY AGENT

Well, I know you probably didn't see this week's rankings. So let me be the first to say: congratulations! Your show is a hit.

ME

A hit? What were we? Ninety-second?

MY AGENT

Ninety-third, actually.

ME
And how is that a hit?

MY AGENT
Because who cares about what the ranking is? (A) it's all about demographics; and (C) the people who need to see the show have seen the show and they call me every five minutes because they love you and they want to be in business with you.

ME
Who are these people?

MY AGENT
Never you mind. You just concentrate on getting well. Get out of town, go on vacation. Because come June first, my friend, things'll start popping.

ME
You mean we'll be in production on our series?

MY AGENT
God, only as a last resort.

ME
What?

MY AGENT
It's not about *this* show. It's not about *this* move. It's all about the move *after* this move.

ME
What?

MY AGENT
Chill for the next few months. Then

we decide if you stay at this studio or
trade up.

                    ME
But I still want to do more episodes of our
series.

                MY AGENT
My advice: get to work on the Percocet.
I'm running out of prescription pads.

                                    CUT TO:

Our overall deal with the studio is up June 1, 1995. Which is,
ironically, around the time that the network must either order
our show, or cancel it outright. We wrapped production on our
show February 17, 1995. What we have been doing since is
what's known as letting our deal run out.

The theory is as follows: with a show on the air—anyone's air,
even a new unwatched network's air—you're sought after by all
the studios, and even some brand-new studios with hugely
famous owners. So while you wait for the network to make up its
mind, you take meetings, you have lunches, you hang around
the house a lot with dirty hair and five o'clock shadow.

For years, I have wondered about the huge numbers of
people that throng the city in the middle of the day—driving
around, shopping, lingering over lunch, playing tennis, hanging
out at the beach. This city is jammed in the middle of the day
with all sorts of layabouts and lazybones. This is not Manhattan,
whose downtown streets in the middle of the day are neutron-
bomb quiet. LA is busy all day long, the golf courses and tennis
courts and gyms and supermarkets and shops filled to capacity
by midmorning. Who are these people? I have wondered. I have
finally figured it out. They are all television producers, waiting to
hear from the network. They are all letting their deals run out.

                                    CUT TO:

INT. MY PLACE—DAY

Morning. I have just returned from a three-week trip through Central America. I am drinking coffee in my underwear, staring at a pile of unpacked luggage.
I've lost track of time: it's May, network scheduling season.

> MY AGENT
>
> Hi. Welcome back.

> ME
>
> Thanks.

> MY AGENT
>
> Did you have a good time?

> ME
>
> I had a great time, thanks.

> MY AGENT
>
> Great. Great.

Pause.

> ME
>
> Um . . . any reason why you called?

> MY AGENT
>
> Of course there's a reason I called. Your show was canceled this morning.

> ME
>
> You're kidding.

> MY AGENT
>
> I am? I don't think I am. I think I'm serious.

> ME
>
> Damn.

> MY AGENT
>
> May I be honest with you? Your show did

not deserve to be canceled. Some shows
deserve to be canceled. Your show did not
deserve to be canceled. May I be honest
with you? *I wish the network ill.* Seriously.
I wish them *ill.* And I wish that on people
very very rarely if ever.

                    ME
Damn.

              MY AGENT
Stop saying damn. Say fuck. It'll feel
better.

                    ME
Fuck.

              MY AGENT
Feel better?

                    ME
No.

              MY AGENT
I told you that you wouldn't. Look, don't
wallow in this. I have a call I have to take.
Stay by the phone.

                              CUT TO:

INT. OUR OFFICE—LATER

*Dan and I are deep in thought. We have been mulling
over a number of offers from competing studios. As we
near the official end of our deal, and with this
morning's news still rattling around our heads, we try
to divine a next move.*
SFX: Phone rings.
The PA enters, nervously. He knows what's been going

on, and he knows who would be the first to go in the event of a cancellation.

PA
(nervous)
Front office on line one, from New York.

It's an executive from our studio, calling from New York, where, for some reason still unclear to me after five years in the business, the various network heads travel every year from Los Angeles to announce their fall television show schedules, which means the various studio heads and various agents and various producers also travel from Los Angeles to lobby and cajole and make last-minute pleas. It could all be accomplished at one-half the cost if everyone decided, "Hey, we're all in Los Angeles, let's just stay in Los Angeles," which wouldn't make the owners of the St. Regis, Regency, Carlyle, and Four Seasons hotels very happy, but would make their employees very happy, since no one likes to have a bunch of nervous wrecks in fancy suits screaming "Where's the Ty Nant water?!" at them for two weeks straight.

PA (CONT'D)
Aren't you going to get it?

I nod and answer the phone.

ME
So we're canceled?

STUDIO EXEC
Who said that?

ME
The network did. At their press
conference.

                    STUDIO EXEC
That's what they said then. What they say
now is very different.

                        ME
What do they say now?

                    STUDIO EXEC
It's unclear.

                        ME
Look, are we canceled or not?

                    STUDIO EXEC
Absolutely not.

                        ME
Really?

                    STUDIO EXEC
Listen, who knows, really? Canceled? Not
canceled? Maybe a midseason back order
for thirteen? I'm not in the predicting
business. I *was* in the predicting business,
but then, know what? *I got out of the
predicting business.*

                        ME
I think there's something wrong with this
phone. I couldn't quite understand a word
you said.

                    STUDIO EXEC
Listen, I predict they order thirteen
episodes as a backup.

                        ME
When?

                    STUDIO EXEC
I predict in two weeks.

ME

Oh.

STUDIO EXEC

Got a sec? Think with me a minute.
Hypothetical time. Say they don't order
the show. Say your show's canceled. Now
what?

ME

Now what, what?

STUDIO EXEC

Now what where do you guys go? Where's
the fit? Do you know where the fit is? I'll
be honest with you. I know you've been
taking meetings around town. But where's
the fit? Let me tell you where *I* think the
fit is.

ME

It's here. I'm having it.

STUDIO EXEC

Let me call you back.

CUT TO:

We sit in our office for another hour or two. Our show, our
little show, has been a difficult case from the start. We shot the
pilot episode a year ago, for one network, they passed on it, a
start-up network bought it and ordered twelve more episodes,
which we shot in the autumn and early winter, it premiered in
January, ran until a week ago, canceled this morning, maybe
uncanceled this afternoon. . . .

In my wallet, stapled to my driver's license, I have an organ
donor's card, which means, in the clearest possible terms, that if
I'm in a hideous car wreck (which in Los Angeles is a matter of
living here long enough), the hospital personnel are empowered,

upon my death, to scavenge my body for usable organs. There's also a box marked DO NOT RESUSCITATE which instructs the hospital personnel on what to do if I'm brain-dead but still clinging to life. I have checked the box. "Do not resuscitate" is my motto, in life, love, and business. It isn't much, but it's mine. If I knew Latin, I'd have a coat of arms made up.

CUT TO:

INT. OUR OFFICE—DAY

Thick clouds of cigar smoke.
SFX: Phone rings.
I answer it myself for two reasons: (a) because I'm closer to it and (b) because the PA and the other office employees are all off xeroxing their résumés.

MY AGENT
I have great news.

ME
We got an order?

MY AGENT
No.

ME
We're canceled, and that's that, it's over, we can move on?

MY AGENT
No.

ME
What, then?

MY AGENT
Keep guessing. I like seeing how your mind works.

                    ME

What?

                 MY AGENT

The good news is that the studio called
me and made an offer to extend your deal
two more years. At what I can only
describe, after thirty years in this
business, as a *serious escalation of monies*.

                    ME

How serious?

                 MY AGENT

First let me caution you against your
tendency to equate money with happiness.

                    ME

How serious?

                 MY AGENT

Your life, your life*style*, is something that
you and you alone can make into
happiness. And no amount of money will
alter that.

                    ME

How serious?

                 MY AGENT

Life is to be lived, here, on earth. Not in
some bloodless ledger book.

                    ME

How serious?

*My agent then mentions a figure that is large and
round and Rubenesque. Dan and I look at each other.*

                ME (CONT'D)

Why?

Why what?

Why did they call and offer to re-up us at
such a premium? We just got canceled.
We failed.

In the first place, you did not get canceled.
You *maybe* got canceled. In the second
place, even if you *did* get canceled, by
getting canceled, you've proved that
you're players in the big game, and (C),
don't ever say we've failed to me again.
You did not fail. It was a good show that
deserved better from its auspices. And
fourth, the reason that they re-upped you
at such a premium is because you have
unquestionably the finest agent in this or
any other universe, and rather than draw
this out any longer, let me just say, you're
welcome, it was my pleasure.

CUT TO:

The network calls later to say that while our show is not on
the fall schedule, it is not canceled. They need two weeks to
decide up-or-down, yes-or-no.

"Do not resuscitate," I think to myself. But it's no use. In
Hollywood—in *my* Hollywood, anyway—that's a useless motto.
This business is about lingering, about near death, brain death,
and last-minute doses of adrenaline and shock pads. Projects go
from here to there to life to dormancy because they linger,
because they survive. And out here, just surviving gets you a
serious escalation of monies.

CUT TO:

EXT. HARVARD BUSINESS SCHOOL—DAY

I am back in my hometown, Boston, to watch an old friend graduate from Harvard Business School. We still have not heard from the network. At the many graduation parties I attend, no less than two dozen young, newly minted MBAs saunter over to me and announce, with charming arrogance, that they are moving to Los Angeles to get involved in the entertainment industry. I smile and encourage each one with great intensity. "Fuck 'em," I think to myself, "let 'em learn the hard way."

As the students approach the dais, spread out on the splendid lawn in the middle of a beautiful New England spring morning, a noise snaps me back to present day.
SFX: Cell phone chirps.
I answer it, unashamed. I am, after all, at Harvard Business School.

> MY AGENT
> Sorry, kiddo. The show is officially
> canceled.

> ME
> Oh.

> MY AGENT
> What's that noise in the background?

> ME
> I'm at Harvard Business School.

> MY AGENT
> Jeez. Isn't that a little drastic? I mean, you
> still have a very promising career,
> you know.

ME

No, not that. I'm here watching a friend
graduate.

MY AGENT

You flew all the way back to Boston for
that? Nice guy.

ME

That, and to celebrate my birthday with
some friends.

MY AGENT

Oh! Great! When's your birthday?

ME

Today.

MY AGENT

How old are you?

ME

I just turned thirty.

MY AGENT

Happy birthday!

ME

Some birthday.

MY AGENT

Wait wait wait. You're *thirty*, not fifty. I
know guys who are fifty and have never
had a show on the air, let alone a deal like
you just signed. So just blow out the
candles and shut your trap and get back
here and get another show on the air.
Happy birthday!

I hang up the phone.
SFX: Cell phone chirps.

I answer it.

                    STUDIO EXEC
I assume you heard?

                        ME
Yeah.

                    STUDIO EXEC
Look, I'm sorry. We did what we could.
They're idiots over there. Idiots.

                        ME
Thanks.

                    STUDIO EXEC
I'm out of town for the weekend. My
daughter just graduated from Harvard
Business School and so I'm in Boston—

                        ME
You're at the HBS graduation?

                    STUDIO EXEC
Yeah. Why?

                        ME
So am I.

                    STUDIO EXEC
What?

*I stand up on my chair and scan the crowd. I spot the
studio exec in the last row, leaning up against a tree,
talking on his cell phone.*
I wave.

                        ME
  See me waving?

The studio exec looks up, sees me, waves weakly.

_____

STUDIO EXEC

So this call is going to my office in LA,
where my secretary transferred it to your
phone in LA, which bounced it to you
here?

ME

I guess so.

STUDIO EXEC

What a fucking world. By the way, what
are you doing here?

ME

I have a friend who graduates today.

STUDIO EXEC

You have a friend in my daughter's class?
How old are you anyway?

ME

I turned thirty today.

STUDIO EXEC

Fuck you.

ME

I'm serious.

STUDIO EXEC

Fuck you. I was feeling sorry for you but
fuck you.

CUT TO:

INT. AMERICAN AIRLINES FLIGHT 94—DAY

*I'm flying back to LA. I am locked into a conversation
with an elderly woman in the next seat.*

OLD LADY

What do you do?

ME

I'm a television writer.

OLD LADY

How interesting. Have you been doing
it long?

ME

No, not really. About . . .

I start adding up the years in my head.

ME (CONT'D)
(stunned)

Jesus. I've been doing it for over five
years.

OLD LADY

And is Los Angeles your home?

ME

No, not really. I've only lived there
about . . .

I start adding up the years in my head.

ME (CONT'D)
(stunned)

Jesus. I've been living in LA for seven
years.

*My eyes glaze over. The old lady leaves me to my
thoughts.*

CUT TO:

Something occurred to me on that plane ride: I grew up in
Los Angeles. I arrived at a very young twenty-three, and I arrive
this day a still-young but wiser thirty.

It's all blurred: film school, getting an agent, *Cheers* . . . it's all
blurred except for *our* show, which failed in only the narrowest

sense, but succeeded in so many others: we learned a lot, we showed whomever we needed to show that we could do it, and I became whatever passes these days for an adult. And adulthood—or *my* adulthood, anyway—is characterized by a sense that life is an episodic comedy: funny little scenes connected by the thinnest tissue of meaning, characters you like and want to spend time with, and a big payoff at the end.

Screenwriting format allows for two ways to end a scene: the "fade" and the "dissolve." The "fade" is final: fade to blackness, the picture slowly transforms to a solid black frame. The "dissolve" is what we use in television. It's more forgiving. A "dissolve" is a transition between one thing and the next, between scenes, say, or moments in a script. When you "fade," you "fade *out*." When you "dissolve," you "dissolve *to*."

INT. MY PLACE—DAY

Late afternoon. I've just arrived from the airport. I set my bags down, greet my dog, flip through the mail, pour myself a beer, and walk out onto my balcony.
SFX: Phone rings.
I know who it is. I let the machine pick up.

DISSOLVE TO:

Santa Monica, California

DUTTON   ℗ **PLUME**

A SLICE OF LIFE IN AMERICA

☐ **MID-LIFE CONFIDENTIAL** *The Rock Bottom Remainders Tour America with Three Chords and an Attitude.* **Edited by Dave Marsh.** In 1992, fifteen of America's most popular writers—including Stephen King, Amy Tan, Dave Barry, and Barbara Kingsolver—left their day jobs for life on the rock 'n' roll road. They called themselves the Rock Bottom Remainders and spent two weeks barnstorming the East Coast—staying up late, eating junk food, traveling by bus, and actually trying to play and sing before paying audiences, massacring rock 'n' roll classics everywhere. (274591—$12.95)

☐ **BEHIND THE OSCAR** *The Secret History of the Academy Awards* **by Anthony Holden.** At last, the full story of the winners, the losers, the scandals, and the whispers can be told. You'll find out why some of the greatest names in movie history were ignored, and how others were destroyed by the Oscar jinx. Complete with a multitude of award lists and dozens of photos. (271312—$15.95)

☐ **SUMMER OF LOVE** *The Inside Story of LSD, Rock & Roll, Free Love and High Times in the Wild West* **by Joel Selvin.** In the late 1960s and 1970s, the West Coast was the epicenter of rock music. Drawing on more than 200 interviews with all the major players, including Jerry Garcia, Grace Slick, Steve Miller, and David Crosby, the author has assembled the first complete history of this era—a visual "Psychedelic Babylon." "A backstage pass to the wildest, boldest, scariest era in American rock and roll."—Carl Hiaasen (274079—$12.95)

☐ **THE TWENTYSOMETHING AMERICAN DREAM** *A Cross-Country Quest for a Generation* **by Michael Lee Cohen.** This groundbreaking collection of interviews goes beyond the sound bites to reveal the thoughts and souls of Americans in their twenties. This important book surpasses the generalizations to show that much of the negative media hype is unsubstantiated, and that twentysomethings make up a fascinating, diverse group confronting the challenges of the future. (272300—$10.95)

Prices slightly higher in Canada.

DUTTON